This catalogue accompanies an exhibition that was on display at the Duke Gallery of Fine Art, James Madison University, from March 12–April 13, 2019.

Duke Hall Gallery of Fine Art
820 S. Main Street, MSC 7101
Harrisonburg, Virginia 22807
P: 540-568-6407
http://www.jmu.edu/artandarthistory

ISBN 978-1-64516-092-2

Curators: Beth Hinderliter, Maureen G. Shanahan
Designer: Carissa Henriques
Photographer: Elise Trissel
Printer: Progress Printing, Lynchburg, VA
This book was typeset in DIN and printed on Sappi McCoy 100# silk cover and 80# silk text.

IMAGES

Cover: Roy Reeve. Tong traction. French soldier (F.A. Treval) at American Red Cross Military Hospital 2. OHA 80 Reeve 13320A. [1918]. Photograph and black ink on card, 13.5" x 9." National Museum of Health and Medicine, Silver Spring, Maryland.

Pages 4–5: Amina Menia. *Monuments in Exile: An Infinite Page of Marble Writing*, 2019.

Duke Hall Gallery of Fine Art
JAMES MADISON UNIVERSITY.
COLLEGE OF VISUAL AND PERFORMING ARTS
SADAH SCHOOL OF ART | DESIGN | ART HISTORY
CGE CENTER for GLOBAL ENGAGEMENT
ecpad AGENCE D'IMAGES DE LA DÉFENSE
NATIONAL MUSEUM OF HEALTH AND MEDICINE 1862

CONTENTS

Welcome from Katherine A. Schwartz

Director, School of Art, Design and Art History

Welcome to the *Colonial Wounds/Postcolonial Repair* exhibition within the Duke Hall Gallery of Fine Art at James Madison University's School of Art, Design and Art History. The exhibition was co-curated by Maureen G. Shanahan, Professor of Art History and Beth Hinderliter, Associate Professor of Cross Disciplinary Studies.

Dr. Shanahan and Dr. Hinderliter teamed up to create the vision for this exhibition two years ago, by combining their research interests in the power of images for historical documentation and the significant role of artists to bring contemporary relevance to past events. The exhibition addresses the question, "A hundred years on from the First World War (1914–1918), how do we remember—or forget—the immensity of its mass-produced destruction and the violence of its colonial regimes?" The exhibition also features art created by contemporary artist Amina Menia, which shows that colonial-era monuments in Algeria were re-appropriated to commemorate the Algerian War of Independence. In one example, Menia's images drawn directly onto the gallery walls, provides homage to the monuments that were cut off from their bases to be moved.

I encourage you to read the essays in this catalog which provide thoughtful reflections on two different parts of the exhibition. The exhibition includes work on loan from several different collections. Many of the images included in this exhibition have never before been seen in close proximity to each other, and collectively they are appreciated for their historical significance and contemporary cultural relevance.

The exhibition represents our school's commitment to excellence in programming while also inviting us to investigate and critique the important role that artists have in shaping values, challenging stereotypes, and questioning political decisions by examining the impact of war on our lives.

The questions raised by this exhibition address the mission and values of the School of Art, Design, and Art History as we inspire students to be active participants in their own communities. I thank Professors Shanahan and Hinderliter for the enormous energy they provided to navigate the entire exhibition process, including curating, writing essays for the catalog, providing gallery talks, and organizing a series of public lectures and films that engaged participants in thoughtful discourse.

We are fortunate to have consistent support for events in the Duke Gallery of Fine Art through our Dean, Dr. George Sparks, Acting Dean, Dr. Jeff Bush, and Associate Dean, Dr. Sonya Baker in the College of Visual and Performing Arts. Appreciation is extended to Gallery Director, John Ros, and student gallery interns for hundreds of hours devoted to the precision instillation, art transport, packing and unpacking, hosting events, and managing insurance and contracts. And to our faculty and staff who are working to bring the highest quality art experiences to our campus and community, thank you.

Colonial Wounds / Postcolonial Repair

John Ros, Director, Duke Hall Gallery of Fine Art

12 March–13 April 2019
Curated by Maureen G. Shanahan & Beth Hinderliter

Duke Hall Gallery of Fine Art is a space for vibrant cultural discourse. It is a space where the local and academic communities confront contemporary art and our wider cultural experiences. Art confronts. Art energizes. Art breaks barriers between languages and brings us together to be inspired and knowledgeable citizens no matter where we come from.

Gallery experiences should ask much of the viewer. They give us the opportunity to reflect on who we are and to understand better the perspectives and beliefs that have shaped us. Though the physicality of exhibits may come and go, the lasting impression they leave on those who attend them can significantly alter the psychological and internal landscape of what was firmly believed to be the known. Thus, the known shifts and expands to contain many stories and multiple voices.

Colonial Wounds/Postcolonial Repair, co-curated by Maureen G. Shanahan and Beth Hinderliter is one of these important experiences. Looking at colonial violence specifically through French World War I imperialism, the viewer will delve deeply into historical artifacts to contextualize and reframe the scope of colonial destruction. From there, the contemporary artwork of Algerian artist Amina Menia (b. 1976) develops new work upon the destruction of historical imbalances to reclaim power and to mend broken social, economic, and historical structures. The poetic mix of historical and contemporary research creates a lasting experience of intertwining visual conversations.

Special thanks to the National Museum of Health & Medicine in Silver Spring, Maryland and all other collaborators and contributors to this exhibition. Dedication and support such as this help make Duke Hall Gallery of Fine Art's mission—*to present the highest level of fine art experiences and to create an active space for robust discourse of vital issues facing our society*—a reality. *Colonial Wounds/Postcolonial Repair* not only brings outstanding programming to our students and the broader community, but it also builds on our goal to be a visionary leader of fine art for all.

MONUMENTS IN EXILE: AN INFINITE PAGE OF MARBLE WRITING

Amina Menia

With the independence of Algeria in 1962, what is commonly called the Algerian War was officially ended after eight years of armed conflict. In sum, France remained one hundred and thirty-two years in my country. During this long period, France developed many commemorative practices that left lasting marks on the territory. In addition to architecture and urbanism, the transformation of space, language and religion, etc., it created monuments and other commemorative plaques across the country. So much so that at independence, these monuments became problematic for the young Algerian state.

A "war of memories" was to inevitably take the place of the military battle. The commemorative memorials were thus at the heart of this symbolic battle. At the same time that the Europeans and the French settlers or *pieds-noirs* returned to the metropolis, France carried out the repatriation of many of the most significant monuments scattered throughout Algeria.

While the base and trunk of these monuments were generally left in Algeria, the *head* of the monument (most often statues representing political or military figures, winged cherubim or angels, etc.) was repatriated to mainland France and grafted to another monument there. These marble "stumps" thus rehabilitated now serve to glorify the memories of the *pieds-noirs*, members of the right-wing Organisation Armée Secrète and other patriots of "Algérie Française."

In Algeria, the monuments left by France are altered, reinterpreted, and repainted, as if to give rise to a blank page, a bleached palimpsest, now ready to welcome a new narrative.

With their plaques torn off, bodies removed and columns made headless, they nevertheless express the history of resilient cities, almost silenced in the chapter of the colonial night. And even if no one pays attention anymore, these lonely monuments, forgotten there like they are lost baggage, resist being obscured by time. Nevertheless, they remain an urban landmark never neutral, always waiting for a sign of destiny. A marble alphabet for an immemorial history that never ceases being written...

These marble pages are also my language as an artist. My work questions the city, the urban space, its superimposed stories and its marble books, its strata and walls—like palimpsests. I cannot be insensitive to these monuments, even as I may not grasp all the subtleties or all the episodes of their stories. Nevertheless, a part of my story is in these battered monuments, and like a detective or an archaeologist in search of relics that clarify our present, I need these marble pieces to complete the face of my time and look it in the eyes.

FLESH AND STONE

Maureen G. Shanahan
Professor of Art History
James Madison University

What the centennial commemorations of World War I (1914–1918) may have most revealed are ongoing debates over national identities and the contradictions between republican ideals and the longstanding wounds of colonialism. Provoked by a Serbian nationalist who assassinated the heir to the Austrian throne, this "world" war was fought among imperial and colonial powers with a global span—the British, French, Austro-Hungarian, German, Russian and Ottoman—empires that have all since disintegrated. In recent decades, new histories have emerged about the role of colonial subjects, the Versailles Peace Treaty's contradictory aim to expand democracy while also quelling demands for autonomy and democratic processes, the psychic and social battles that ensued for decades after the war, and the war's ongoing geopolitical legacy. Former colonial territories that are now independent nation-states have little motivation to participate in rituals serving the mythos of necessary "sacrifice" for a French "empire," "nation," or "republic" that cast its colonial subjects as children or savages in need of civilizing. Amina Menia's *Enclosed* (2012), shows that many of the colonial-era monuments in Algeria, France's longest held colony from 1830–1962, were re-appropriated to commemorate the Algerian War of Independence (1954–1962). In *Monuments in Exile: An Infinite Page of Marble Writing* (2019), Menia's new installation project created for Duke Hall Gallery of Fine Art, the artist foregrounds monuments whose sculpture was split apart from their bases and taken

LEFT

C. Morel. Facial mold. Quarlerland. 2018.2001.2.1. Late 1916. Plaster, 10" x 7" x 6." National Museum of Health and Medicine, Silver Spring, Maryland.

C. Morel. Facial mold. Quarlerland. 2018.2001.2.2. May 20, 1917. Plaster, 10" x 7" x 6." National Museum of Health and Medicine, Silver Spring, Maryland.

Ecole Dentaire de Paris. Plaster model with full lower dental splint replacing left molars. Dispensaire Militaire 45. (Military Dispensary #45) Ecole Dentaire de Paris (Dental School of Paris). M-550-10134. [1918]. Plaster, metal, 7" x 5" x 3." National Museum of Health and Medicine, Silver Spring, Maryland.

Maureen G. Shanahan is professor of art history at James Madison University in the School of Art, Design and Art History. She is a specialist on French modernism, the visual culture of World War I, trauma theory, and her research investigates gender, sexuality, and colonial discourse.

to France in 1962, leaving independent Algeria with the question of what and whom to commemorate. Contemporary debates in France over national identity and immigration are intertwined with contests over which histories to remember. As historian Pascal Blanchard and others have demonstrated, recent French presidents and politicians still invoke colonialist discourse and colonial nostalgia while at the same time leading anti-immigration movements that target Africans and Muslims.

Organized around the theme of injury, repair, and collective memory, *Colonial Wounds/Postcolonial Repair* juxtaposes the cultural production of artists working during World War I with the contemporary investigations of Algerian artist Amina Menia. Together these artists, working a hundred years apart, address the tensions between imagined wholeness, coherence, or union that contest with fractured bodies and social realities. The war's catastrophic and barbaric destructiveness competed with earlier images of warfare, notions of masculine autonomy, rationality and heroism, and French claims to a "civilizing mission." World War I's new genre of monuments—the Tombs to the Unknown Soldier, the town monuments (Harrisonburg has one), and church memorials, all with their plaques listing the names of the dead—are bound up with their opposite: the unnamed colonial soldiers; and the fragmentation and loss of bodies in the war's mass production of death. These new monuments largely supplanted the heroic equestrian general that had dominated the war monument genre for centuries. So too the mass distribution of photography and film eclipsed residual forms of representing war: grand battle scenes and academic history painting.

World War I saw an explosion of new media and representations of the empire. Photography and film dominated understandings of the war and competed with older media. In 1915, the French Army created photography and film divisions to disseminate an "official view" of the war. In addition, commercial periodicals such as *L'Illustration,* published in Paris from 1843 to 1944, incorporated photography alongside reproductions of pastel, painting, lithograph, and other media by academic artists such as Georges Scott, Lucien Jonas, and François Flameng, whose work was promoted and collected by France's Musée de l'Armée (Magnon 2014, 114–121). War photography albums, such as *Der Grosse Krieg in Bildern (The Great War in Pictures*), published in Berlin with captions in six languages, visualized the war in terms of portraits of generals, politicians, and notables, diplomatic meetings, new weaponry, staged scenes of troops in formation, the daily life of soldiers, and the towns and villages near fronts in France, Eastern Europe, the Middle East, and Africa. Colonial subjects appear in training, in their battalions, as ethnographic types, and, in the German album, as prisoners of war.

Fig. 1
Jules Gervais-Courtellemont. *Tirailleurs Algériens*. (Algerian Infantrymen). Autochrome photograph published in *Les Champs de Bataille de la Marne*. Paris: L'Edition Française Illustrée, 1915, page 47. 18 x 24cm (image only) (7.08" x 9.44").

Auguste and Louis Lumière, who invented film in 1895, and the autochrome, a color photography process, in 1907, were major contributors to the new visual environment. The Lumière autochrome technique, adopted by many other artists, was used to depict the global campaign. In one autochrome we see a group of Algerian recruits: infantrymen (*tirailleurs*) in their blue military jackets and uniforms "posed by the author" and "ready to depart for the front" (Fig. 1). They represent some of the 600,000 recruits from France's empire who served as soldiers and workers in the war (Deroo 2013, 138–39). The photographer, Jules Gervais-Courtellemont (1863–1931), published the photograph in his war album, *Les Champs de Bataille de la Marne* (*The Battlefields of the Marne*). The album sequences the photographs in order to tell a story of the war leading to the First Battle of the Marne, an early, decisive battle in September 1914 that blocked the German advance to Paris. The caption tells us that the men are diverse in their origins: Kabyle, a Berber-speaking people, from the city of Djurdura (about one hundred kilometers east of the capital, Algiers) and from the Aurès Mountains to the east, southern Arabs, and farmers from the Tell Atlas Mountains, which run parallel to Algeria's Mediterranean coast. Some have French flags tucked in their coats as they all stand in formation on a hill that descends behind them. On the horizon, we see the Mediterranean Sea and their route to France and to battle.

Fig. 2
Georges Scott (1873-1943). *La Breche* (The Breach), later known as *L'Effet d'un obus dans la nuit* (The Effect of a Shell at Night). Ink and Pastel with gouache highlights. 66cm x 101cm (25.9" x 39.7"). Paris, Musée de l'Armée. Published in *L'Illustration* (29 May 1915).

However, battles could not be directly represented and much of the war was not visible: camera equipment was heavy and not suitable for the front lines or nighttime battles; and censorship contained the sight of the massification of death and dismemberment. Sometimes older media seemed more authentic than photography's staged scenes. In April 1915, before censorship set in, the artist Georges Scott created an ink and pastel drawing entitled *La Breche* (*The Breach*), later re-titled *L'Effet d'un obus dans la nuit* (*The Effect of a Shell in the night*) (Fig. 2). Published a month later in *L'Illustration*, the picture depicts the explosive power of a bomb hitting the front lines. At left, a soldier is knocked off balance by the blast whose bright light casts him in silhouette and illuminates the remaining figures. Another soldier at the center of the scene seems to have been thrust forward and upward by the force of the blast. His broken rifle flies up above him, while his severed arm and leg are flung in opposing directions toward rows of troops on either side. Attributed to "a combatant at the Belgian front," the caption describes the explosion as making "a breach in *their* ranks...one could see bodies, legs, arms flying in the air and swirling before falling on the survivors who kept marching. *Our* machine-gunners then mowed them down" (emphasis added). Scott's dramatic scene envisioning the moment when bodies are torn asunder is exceptional in his work and in published images. It may have been possible only because those bodies are meant to be understood as "theirs," not "ours."

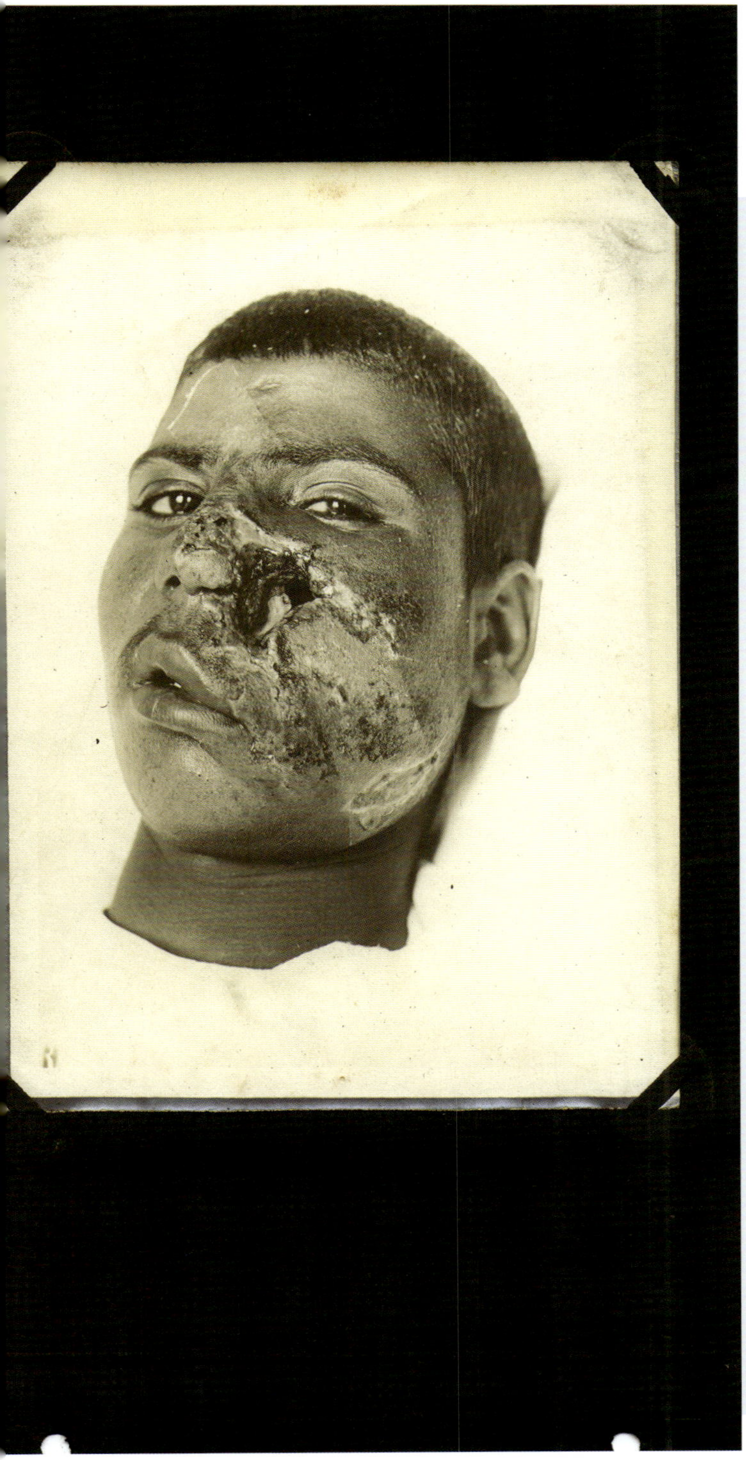

Fig. 3
Unknown photographer. *Ahmed Bouziane*. April 29, 1916. Ward 249, no. 4747. 10.5" x 7". Leach Scrapbook, 1914-1918. National Museum of Health and Medicine. OHA 213.5, image 38.

Dismemberment and disfiguration occurred in massive numbers due to the new technologies of war, and the scale of injuries compelled medical advancements and innovations. Reconstructive surgeries sutured together horrible facial breaches, prosthetic limbs were configured for the labor (and class) of the veteran, machine therapies and electric shock treatments served to regain flexibility and use of muscle movement, and, in some contexts, rest cures, hypnosis, and even psychotherapy became therapies for the traumatized mind. Of the many new wounds produced by the war, it was disfiguration due to explosions and burns from gassing that could perhaps most converge physical and psychic damage. Artists working for medical doctors sought to document and understand the wounds as well as the processes for surgical repair and reconstruction.

Where Gervais-Courtellemont and Scott produced a body of images for public consumption and distribution, often unknown medical artists and photographers generated another body of images for private medical study. In one case, an American doctor stationed in France created a photography album of those with damaged faces, including a young Algerian man, Ahmed Bouziane (Fig. 3). The date of the photograph, April 29, 1916, suggests that Bouziane may well have suffered his wounds in the Battle of Verdun, the largest and longest battle of the war that had begun in late February and lasted into November.

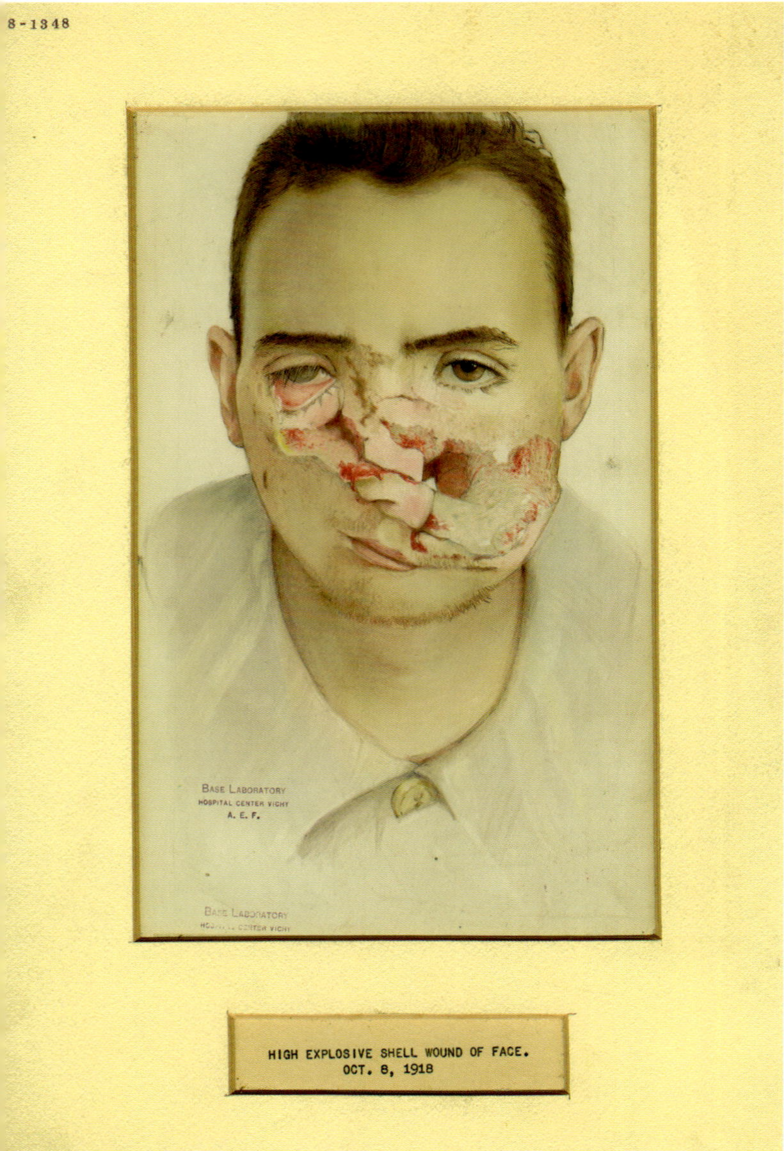

Fig. 4
Corp. John Butler AEF. Pvt. Alex G. Nesbit, 363d Infantry, Dijon, France. High explosive shell wound of face, Oct 8, 1918. OHA 229.27.20. color pencil. 16" x 11". National Museum of Health and Medicine, Silver Spring, Maryland.

Fig. 5 (opposite)
T Corp. John Butler AEF. Pvt. Alex G. Nesbit, 363d Infantry, Dijon, France. High explosive shell wound of face, Oct 29, 1918. OHA 229.27.21. color pencil. 12.5" x 11" National Museum of Health and Medicine, Silver Spring, Maryland.

Apparently propped up in bed in a seated position, he gazes left out of the corner of his eyes toward the photographer, whose tripod and camera must have been set up to the side of the patient's bed. The framing of the patient in a hospital gown and against bedsheets is such that his head and neck seem to float in a field of overexposed flattened whiteness. The camera captures a three-quarter view of his face aimed to position his shocking wound and the gaping hole next to his nose at the center of the image. The wounds were probably caused by a high explosive shell that burned across his face from the left side of his nose down to his chin, peeling off skin, puncturing the bone and cartilage, and causing the left side of his mouth to droop.

What were the medical treatments and post-war destiny of colonial soldiers like Bouziane? Known in France as the *gueules cassés* or broken faces, soldiers wounded in the face suffered a "double violence" to their bodies and to their sense of self or identity, as Sophie Delaporte has argued. Artillery shells projected into trenches could render a man unrecognizable, require multiple surgeries, and impact their intimate and familial relations. In a pair of color pencil drawings of a white soldier with wounds similar to Bouziane, the military artist, Corp. John Butler, AEF, shows an American soldier, Alex G. Nesbit, with his wounds still fresh on October 8, 1918, and then after surgery on October 29, 1918 (Figs. 4 and 5). Even with his skin sutured together, the body cannot be returned to its

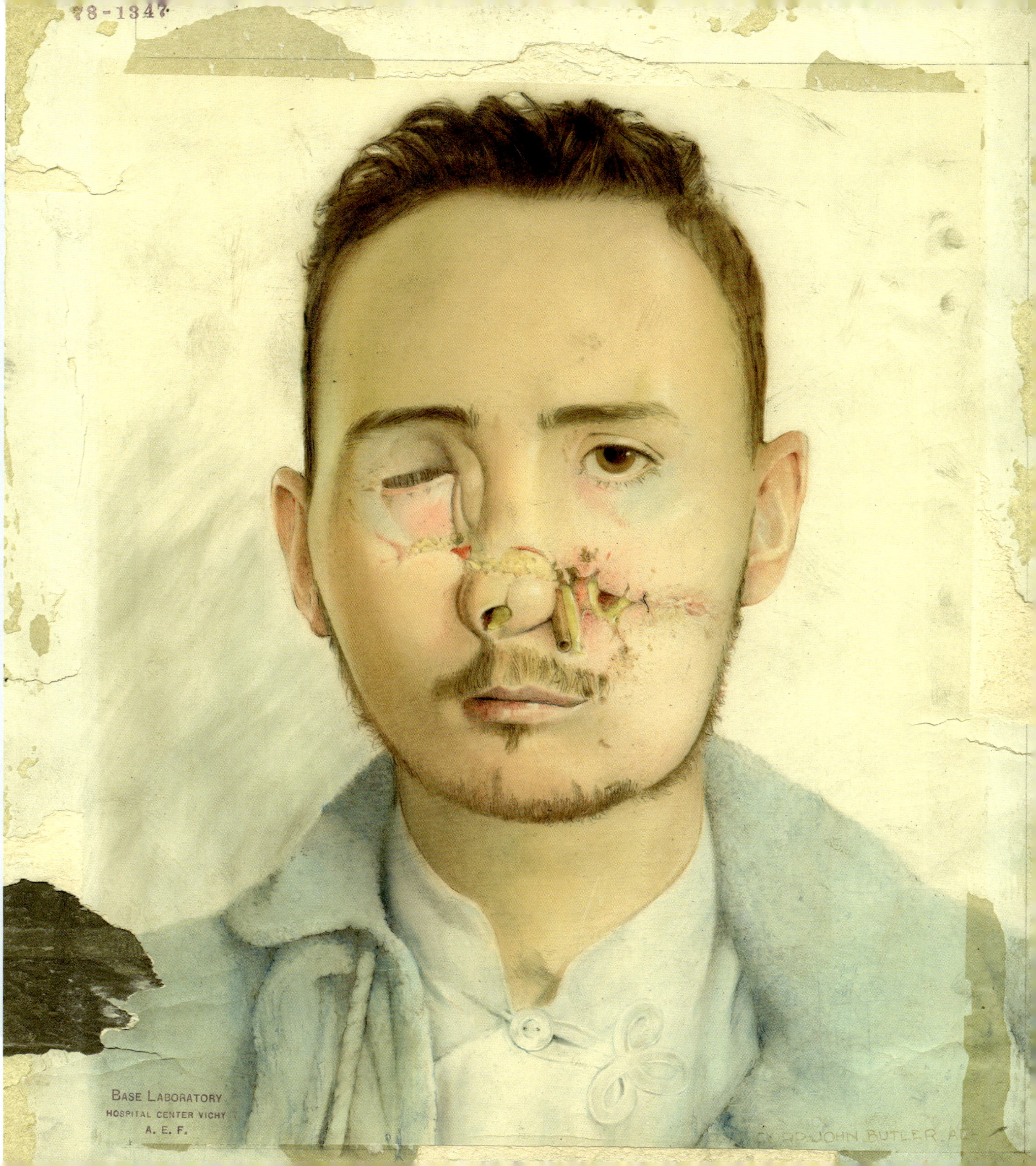
78-1347
BASE LABORATORY
HOSPITAL CENTER VICHY
A. E. F.
RP. JOHN BUTLER

Fig. 6
Helen Ely Richardson. Diagram of Facial Reconstruction Surgery. Alfred Dube, serial No. 24267. Sketch I: 2/13/19. U.S. General Hospital No. 2, Fort McHenry, MD. OHA 229.20.02. Ink and red pencil. 10" x 13". National Museum of Health and Medicine, Silver Spring, Maryland.

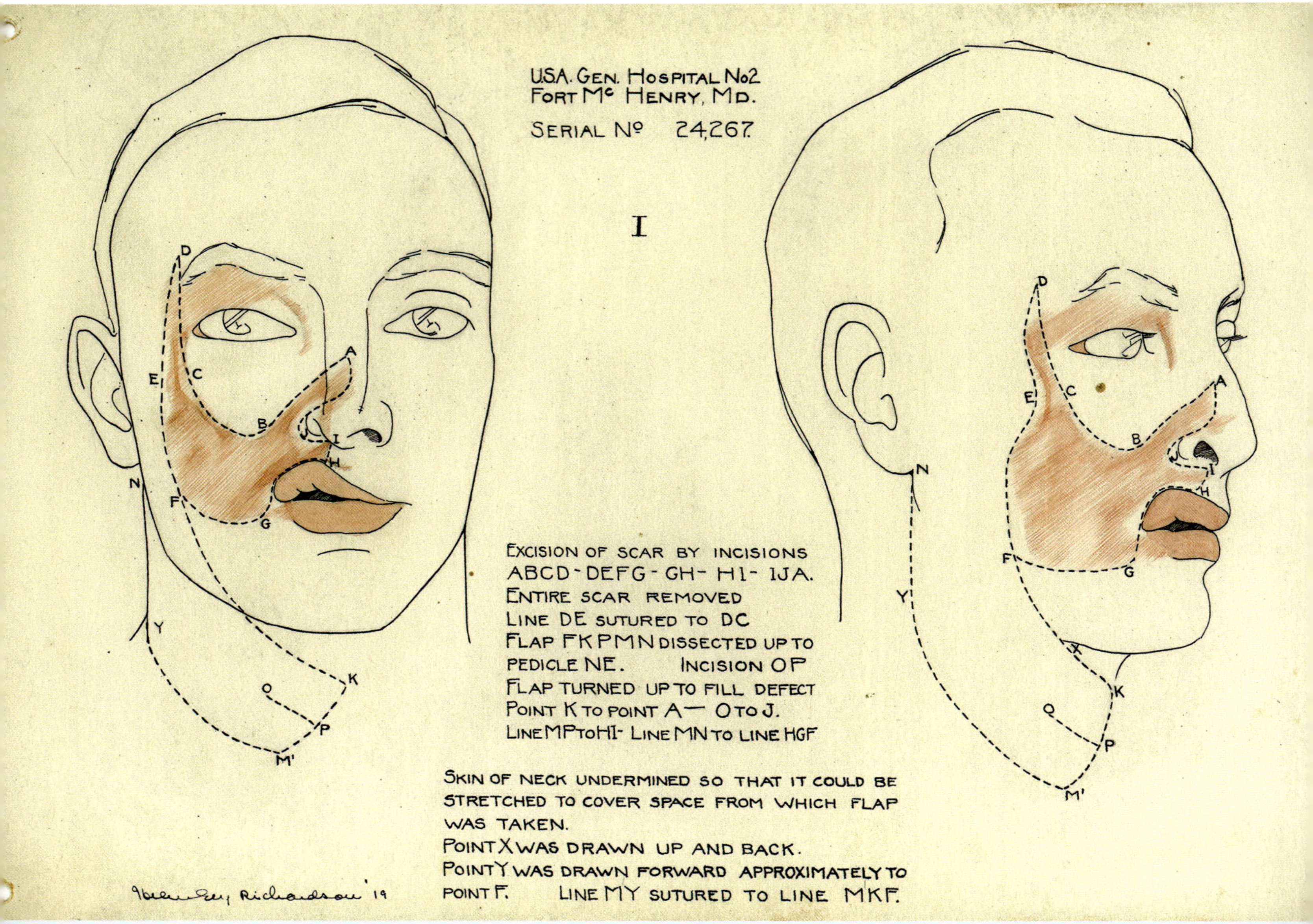

Fig. 7
Unknown photographer. Front and sice view of unknown African-American soldier with facial wounds. [1918]. 8.5″ x 14″. OHA 364.001.007, page 76 of 251-page album. National Museum of Health and Medicine, Silver Spring, Maryland.

original state: the vision out of Nesbit's right eye is occluded and a nasal stent or airpipe protrudes from the side of his nose. An ink and pencil diagram by Helen Ely Richardson outlines the steps of a surgical plan for facial reconstruction of one Alfred Dube, a surgical plan relevant to Bouziane's wounds (Fig. 6). Where Nesbit's wounds and surgery took place in France during the last month of the war before the November 11 Armistice, Dube's surgery was planned for February 1919 after his repatriation to the United States, an indication of the duration and complexity of the process. An American Red Cross film of artist Anna Coleman Ladd shows her working in her Paris studio with facial molds on the wall behind her. In addition to the molds, she made masks for soldiers to wear in public, evidence of the limits of surgery and a desire to protect the viewer from the sight of horrific disfiguration.

But what is the evidence of similar surgical care and facial masks for African soldiers? Would Bouziane have received the series of surgeries that Nesbit, Dube, and others received? Would his surgeries have continued in Algeria after his repatriation as occurred for Dube or as was demanded by French veterans in the interwar years? How did the classicizing logic of Ladd's facial masks inform their production (if at all) for colonial soldiers? One French Army film depicting disabled soldiers presents an individual French veteran wearing a prosthetic right arm to show his ability to farm, while a clip of African soldiers from the Jardin Colonial envisions them as a group, many missing limbs, one with his head bandaged, but none with prosthetics, yet still expected to work the land. Whatever surgeries Bouziane received, the results were likely to have left scars similar to those evident in the photographs of an unknown African-American soldier whose front and profile views show permanent scarification on his left cheek (Fig. 7). These images raise the question of how the "double violence" of facial wounds intersected with the "double consciousness" of a colonized self.

As we now know, the cultural conditions of sight have a dialectical relationship to human subjectivity. Like the African-American soldiers of the famous 369th Harlem Hellfighters who are represented among the medical images, France's colonial soldiers suffered ongoing discrimination and led postwar battles for citizenship and civil rights. One veteran of the war, Messali Hadj (1898–1974), was motivated by the contradictions between France's republican promises and repressive realities to became the father of the Algerian revolution. But it remains to be studied exactly how colonialist ideology extended to medical treatment, facial reconstruction surgery, the types of prosthetics (if any) the soldiers received, the therapies provided during the war in France and, after 1919, in their homeland. Still unanswered too are questions about the many African workers, largely from Algeria, who came to France in the 1920s and 1930s: how many were veterans; when and how did differential treatment extend to interwar medical practices; and how was the discourse and visualization of medicine bound up in the classicizing aesthetics and new configurations of colonial ideology? In other words, what is the legacy of the wounds of war and colonialism, visible and invisible? The complexity of visibility and memory challenge us to ask what "never again" should we learn and what historical amnesias should we unlearn.

References

Biernoff, Suzannah. 2017. *War and the Aesthetics of Disfigurement*. Ann Arbor, MI: University of Michigan Press.

Delaporte, Sophie. 1996. *Les Gueules Cassés: Les blessés de la face de la Grande Guerre*. Paris: Noêsis.

Deroo, Eric. 2013. "Dying: The Call of the Empire (1913-1918)." 132–139. In Pascal Blanchard, et al, eds. *Colonial Culture in France since the Revolution*. Indiana University Press.

Fogarty, Richard S. 2008. *Race and War in France: Colonial Subjects in the French Army, 1914–1918*. Baltimore, MD: Johns Hopkins University Press.

Magnon, Claire. 2014. "La Grande Guerre exposée à Paris." 114–121. In *Vu du Front: Représenter la Grande Guerre*. Paris: Musée de l'Armée.

Sammons, Jeffrey T. 2014. *Harlem's Rattlers and the Great War: The Undaunted 369th Regiment and the African American Quest for Equality*. Lawrence, KS: University Press of Kansas.

Shanahan, Maureen G. "Battles for Hearts and Minds: The Nogent Mosque during World War I." *African Arts* (forthcoming).

Véry, Laurent. 2010. "1914–1918, the First Media War of the Twentieth Century: The Example of French Newsreels." *Film History: An International Journal* vol. 22, no. 4: 408–425.

Walther, Peter. 2014. *The First World War in Colour*. Köln: Taschen.

Lieut. Albert Moreau. Group of wounded North African soldiers holding postcards. Jardin Colonial, Nogent-sur-Marne. 1916. Photograph. Établissement de Communication et de Production Audiovisuelle de Défense (ECPAD).

Unknown. French colonial soldiers as prisoners of war in a German P.O.W. camp. *Der Grosse Krieg in Bildern*, vol. 4 (1915), 32. Photography album.

Afrikanische Hilfstruppen der Franzosen im Gefangenenlager Zossen-Wünstorf. (Aufgen. 23. 3. 1915.) Copyright by Brown & Dawson.

African colonial troops of the French in the prisoners' camp at Zossen-Wünstorf. (Phot. 23. 3. 1915.)

Tropas auxiliares africanas de los franceses en el campamento de prisioneros de Zossen-Wünstorf. (Tom. 23. 3. 1915.)

Les auxiliaires africains des Français au camp de Zossen-Wünstorf. (Cliché du 23. 3. 1915.)

Truppe ausiliarie africane francesi nel Campo di Concentrazione di Zossen-Wünstorf. (Fot. 23. 3. 1915.)

Tropas auxiliares africanas dos Francezes no accampamento dos prisioneiros á Zossen-Wünstorf. (Tir. no 23. de 3. de 1915.)

32

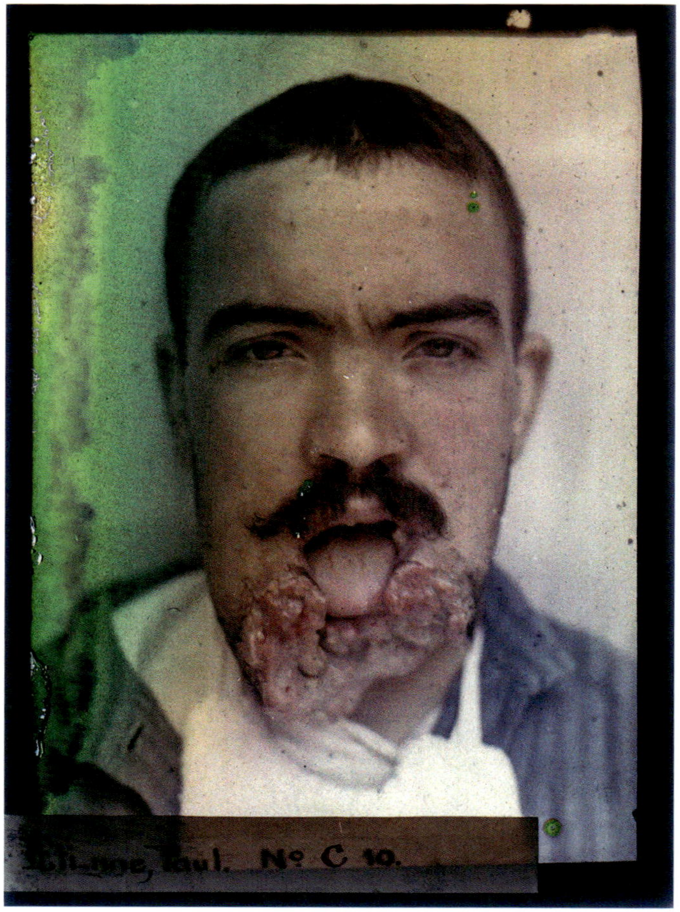

Auguste and Louis Lumière. Paul Etienne, C10. OHA 367.16.004, Box 16. [1918] Color lantern slide, 4 ¾" x 3 ⅝." National Museum of Health and Medicine, Silver Spring, Maryland.

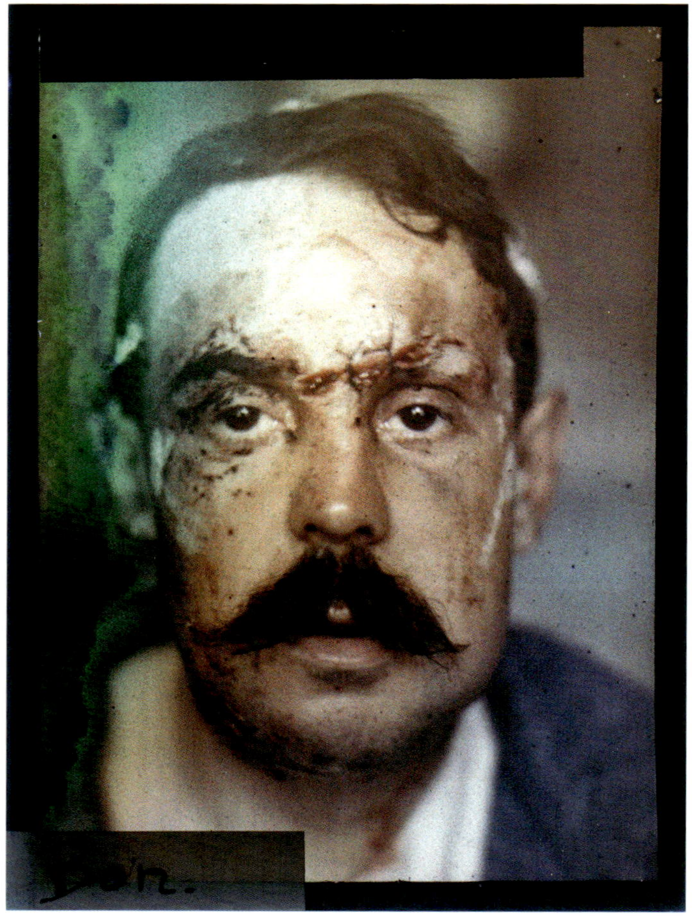

Auguste and Louis Lumière. Jean Bon, F29. OHA 367.16.001, Box 16. [1918] Color lantern slide, 4 ¾" x 3 ⅝." National Museum of Health and Medicine, Silver Spring, Maryland.

Auguste and Louis Lumière. Leonard Legarton, H2, side profile. OHA 367.16.002, Box 16. [1918] Color lantern slide, 4 ¾" x 3 ⅝." National Museum of Health and Medicine, Silver Spring, Maryland.

Auguste and Louis Lumière. Leonard Legarton, H2, frontal view. OHA 367.16.003, Box 16. [1918] Color lantern slide, 4 ¾" x 3 ⅝." National Museum of Health and Medicine, Silver Spring, Maryland.

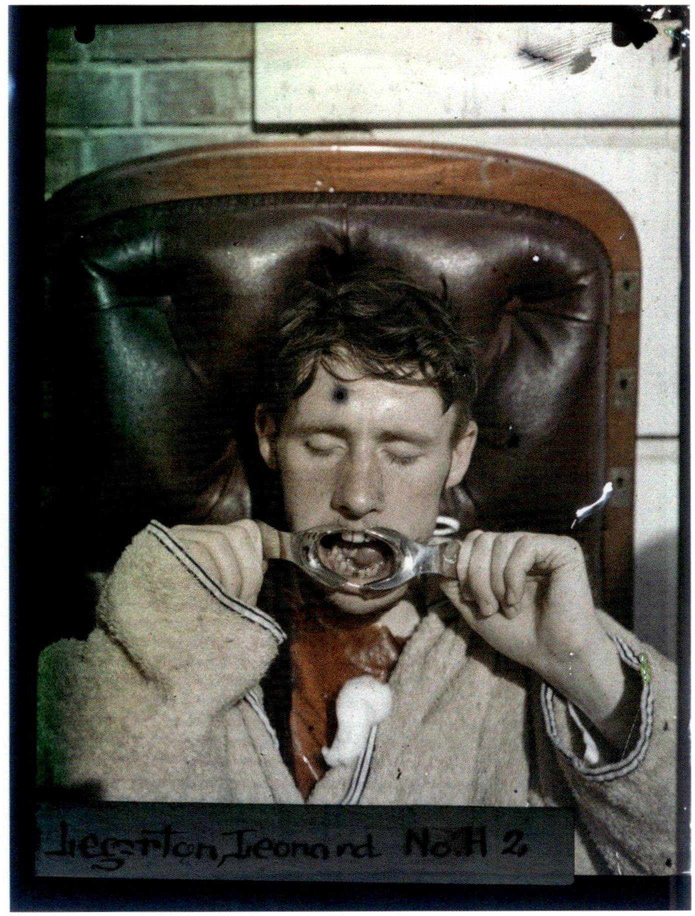

Sgt. J.J. Owens. Chemical Burns. Sgt. Thomas S. Davis. American Red Cross Hospital No. 6. OHA 229.38.25, Box 47, folder 3. October 4, 1918. Watercolor, 18" x 13." National Museum of Health and Medicine, Silver Spring, Maryland.

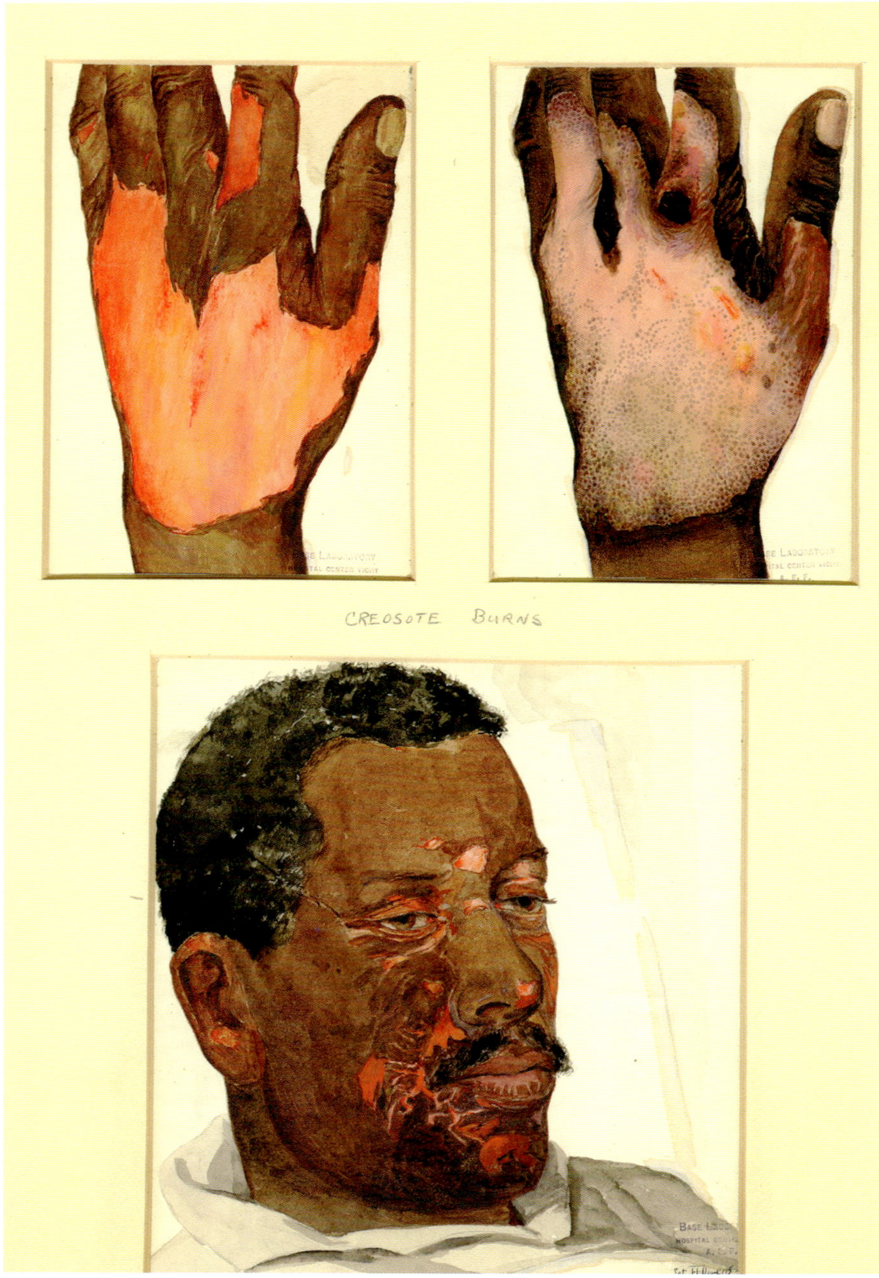

Helen Ely Richardson. Facial reconstruction surgery diagram. John Foster I and II (4/14/1919 & 5/16/1919). 1919. Black ink drawing & red pencil, 10" x 13." National Museum of Health and Medicine, Silver Spring, Maryland.

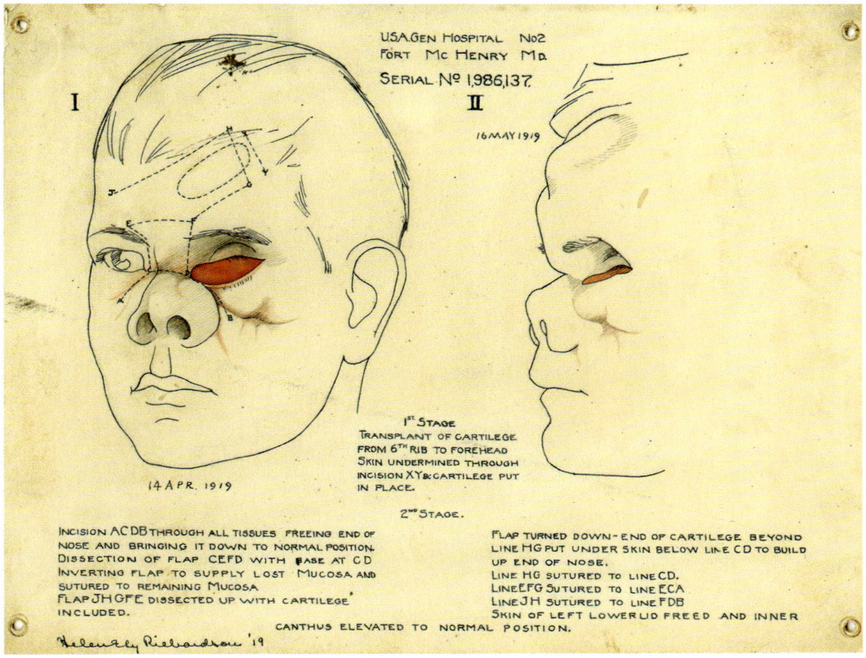

Helen Ely Richardson. Facial reconstruction surgery diagram. John Foster III (5/31/1919). OHA 229.21.07, Box 25, folder 12. 1919. Black ink drawing & red pencil, 10" x 15." National Museum of Health and Medicine, Silver Spring, Maryland.

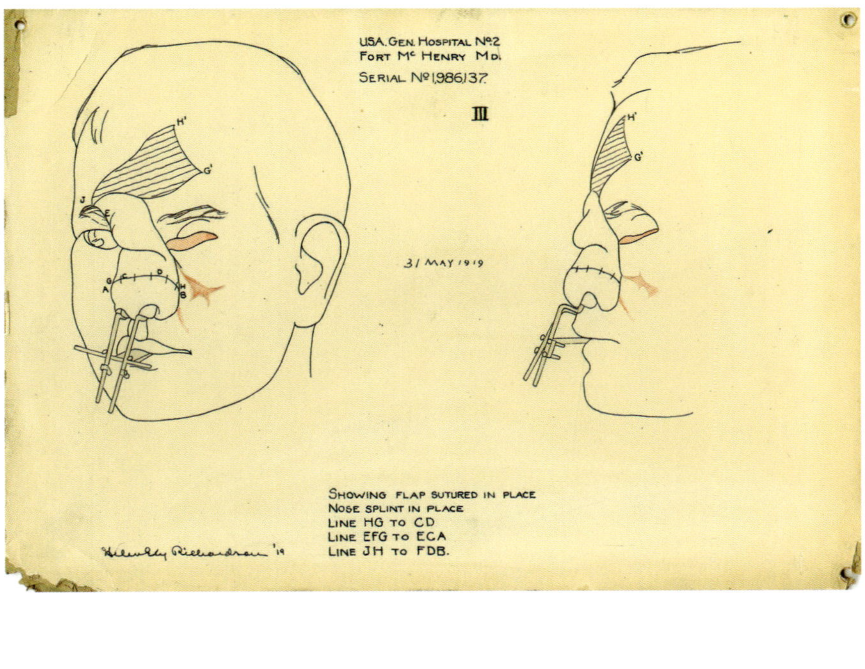

Unknown. Catastrophic Loss of both lower legs. OHA 229.26.22, Box 32, folder 3. [1918]. Watercolor on board, 10.5" x 12." National Museum of Health and Medicine, Silver Spring, Maryland.

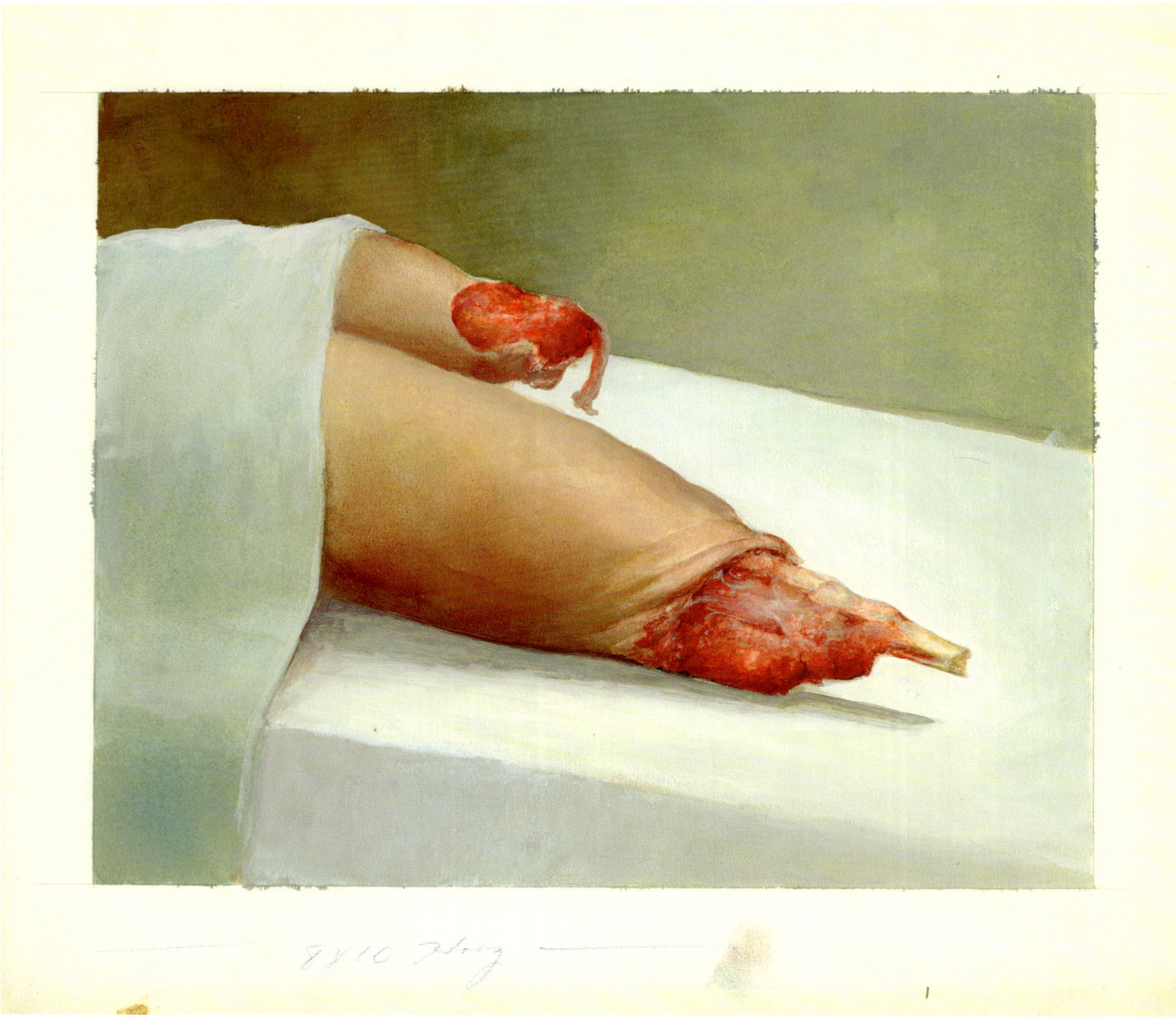

F.E. Prior. #2 of 7 in a series of medical illustrations of thigh amputation. OHA 229.16.21. [1918]. Black ink on paper, 7" x 7." National Museum of Health and Medicine, Silver Spring, Maryland.

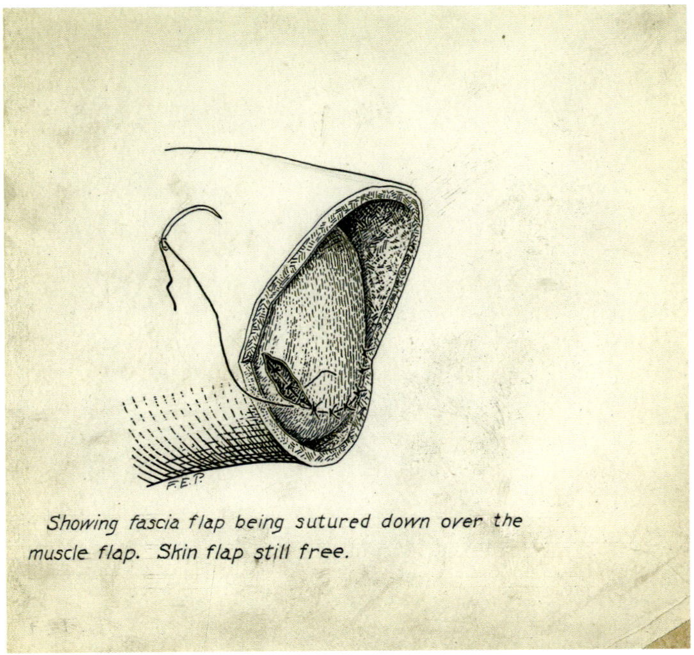

F.E. Prior. #6 of 7 in a series of medical illustrations of thigh amputation. OHA 229.16.21. [1918]. Black ink on paper, 7" x 7." National Museum of Health and Medicine, Silver Spring, Maryland.

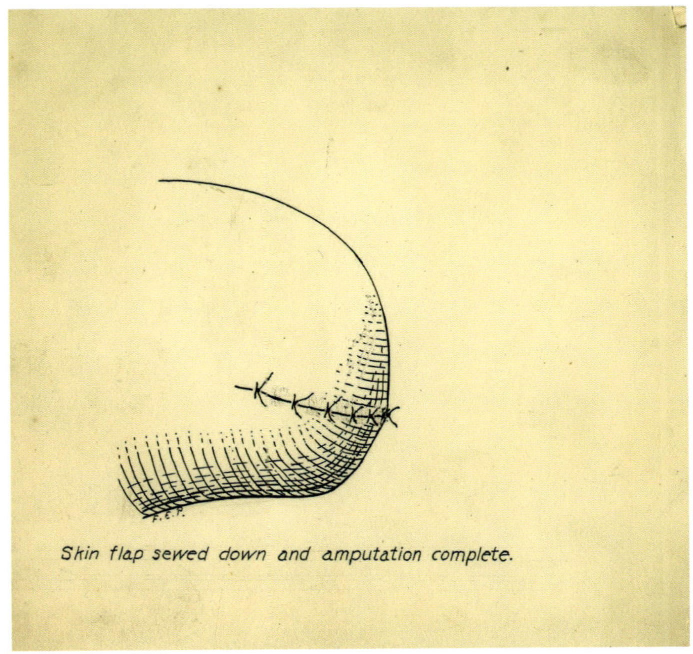

Roy Reeve. Tong traction. French soldier (F.A. Treval) at American Red Cross Military Hospital 2. OHA 80 Reeve 13320A. [1918]. Photograph and black ink on card, 13.5" x 9." National Museum of Health and Medicine, Silver Spring, Maryland.

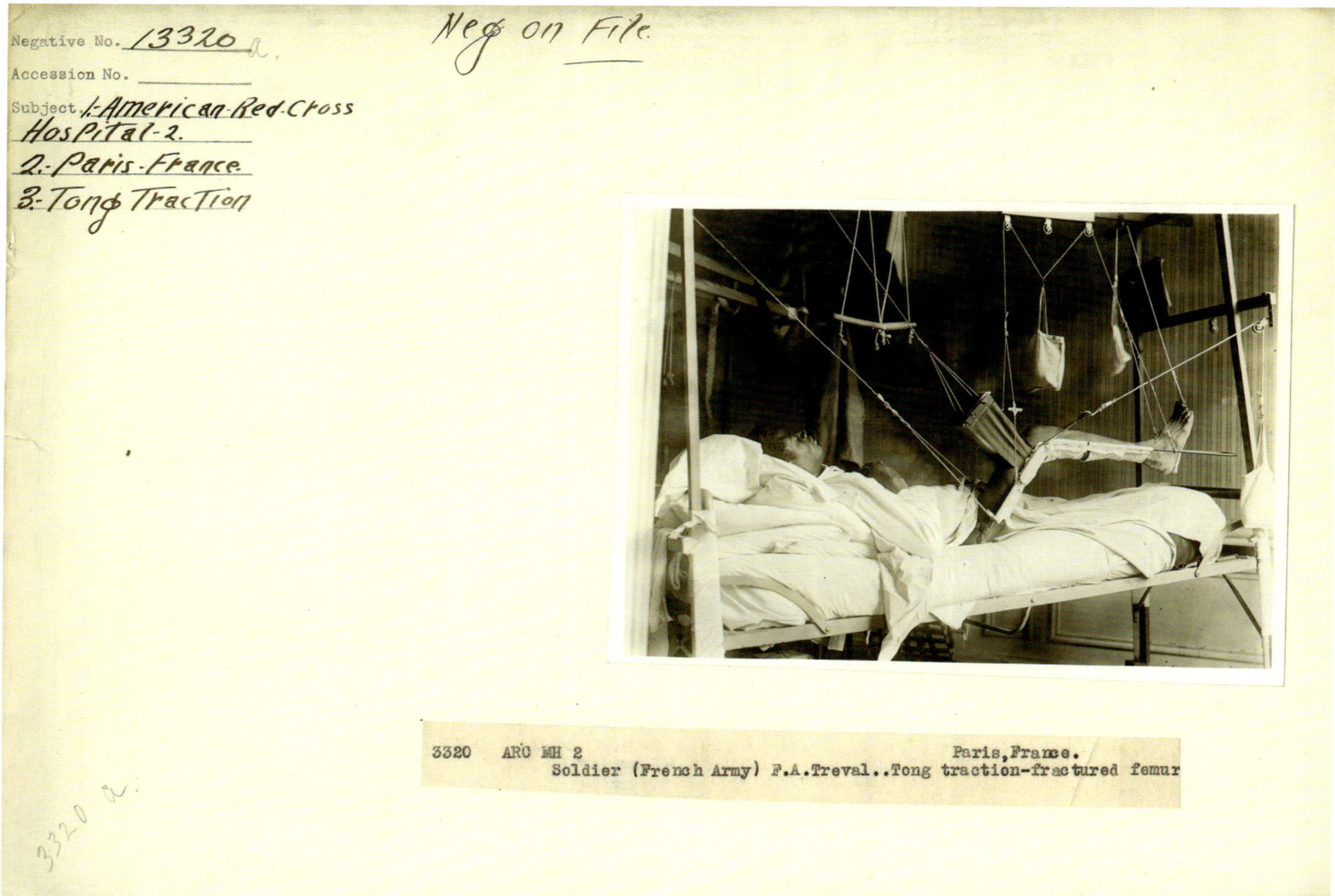

Sgt J.J. Owens. Fractured Femur and Steinman pin. OHA 229.38.16. November 1, 1918. Watercolor, color pencil, black ink, 14" x 17." National Museum of Health and Medicine, Silver Spring, Maryland.

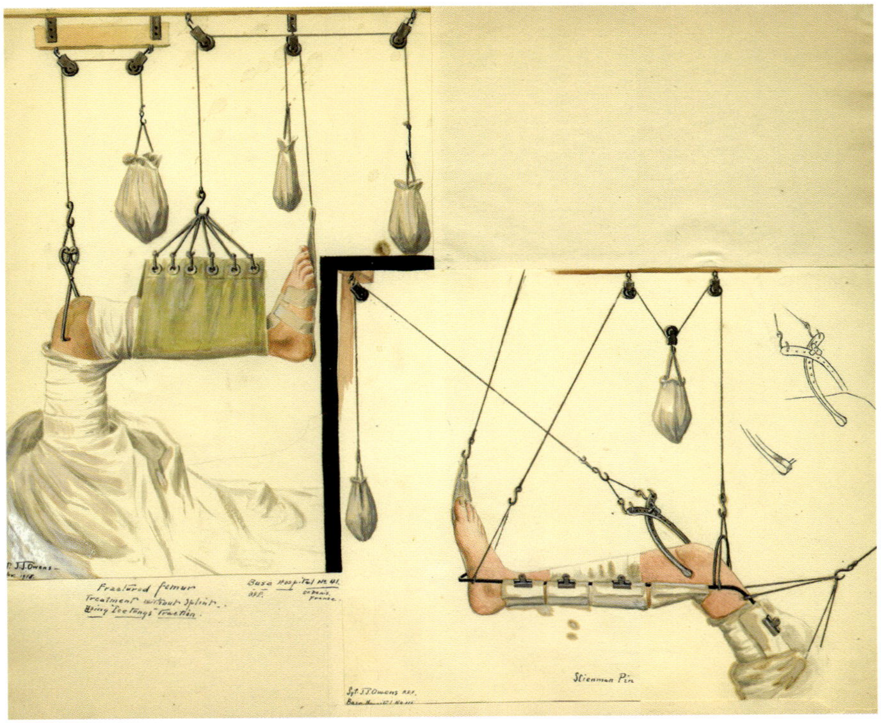

Roy Reeve. Diagram of Balkan Frame. OHA 366. Reeve 68.2. [1918]. Print of glass plate negative on photo paper, 3.5" x 4." National Museum of Health and Medicine, Silver Spring, Maryland.

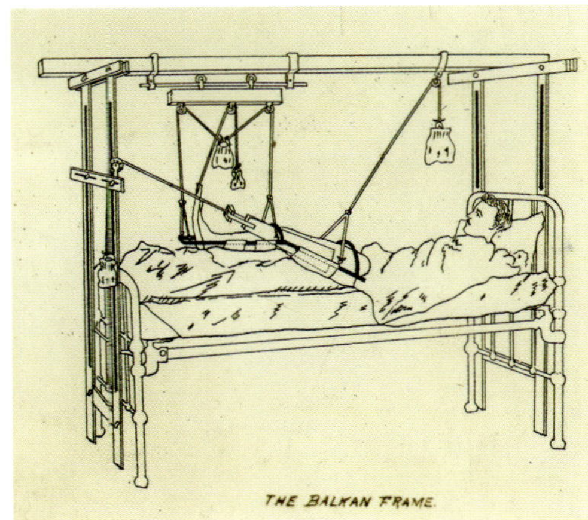

Sgt. J.J. Owens. Side view of right gangrened foot. Sgt Arthur McArthur. 1st C, 369th Infantry. American Red Cross Military Hospital No. 5 & No. 2. OHA 229.39.01, Box 49, folder 4. October 4, 1918. Drawing and watercolor, 13" x 18." National Museum of Health and Medicine, Silver Spring, Maryland.

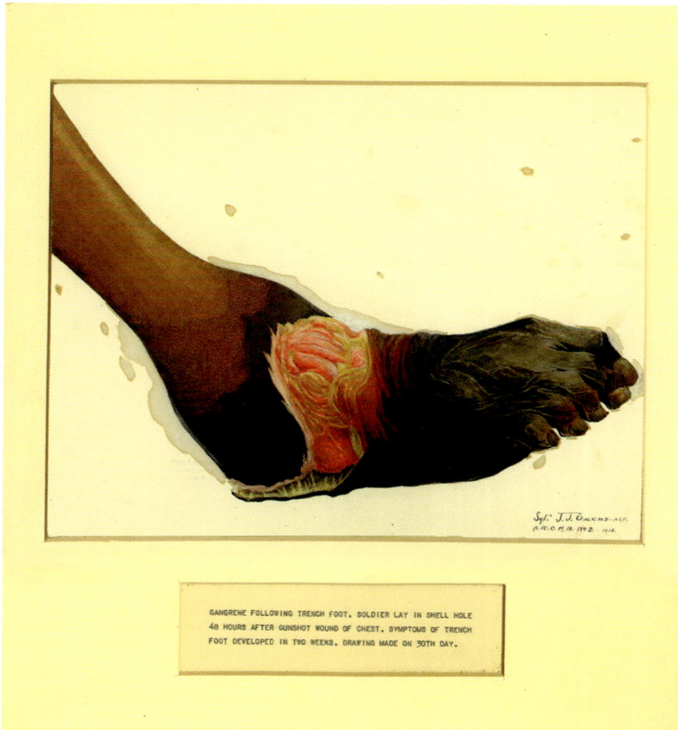

Sgt. J.J. Owens. Front view of left gangrened foot. Sgt Arthur McArthur. OHA 229.38.18, Box 46, folder 12. November 29, 1918. Drawing and watercolor, 17" x 14." National Museum of Health and Medicine, Silver Spring, Maryland.

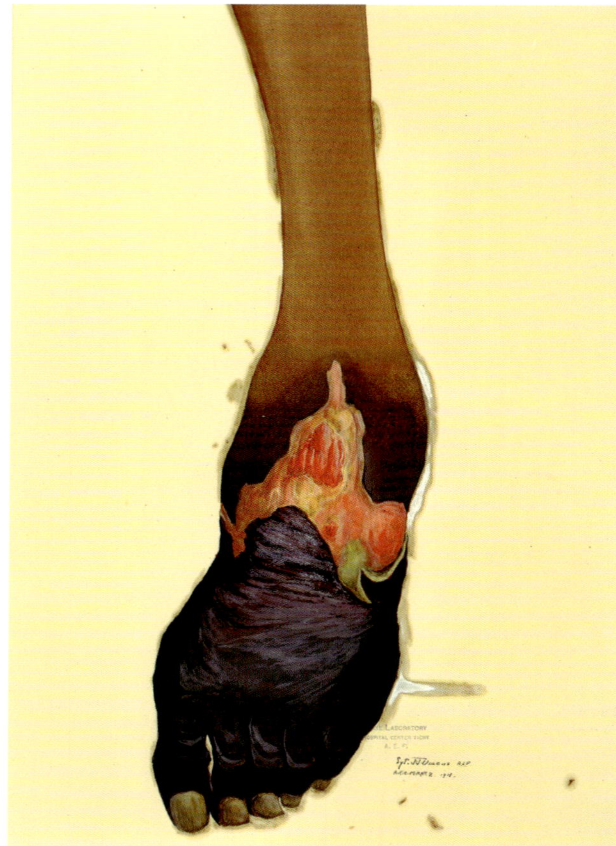

Unknown. Decoration ceremonies. Film 14.18 B 646. 1917-1918. 4-minute extract. Établissement de Communication et de Production Audiovisuelle de Défense (ECPAD), France.

Unknown. Wounded French soldiers. Film 14.18 B 730. 1917. 12-minute newsreel. Établissement de Communication et de Production Audiovisuelle de Défense (ECPAD), France.

C. Morel. Facial mold. Quarlerland. 2018.2001.2.1. Late 1916. Plaster, 10" x 7" x 6."
National Museum of Health and Medicine, Silver Spring, Maryland.

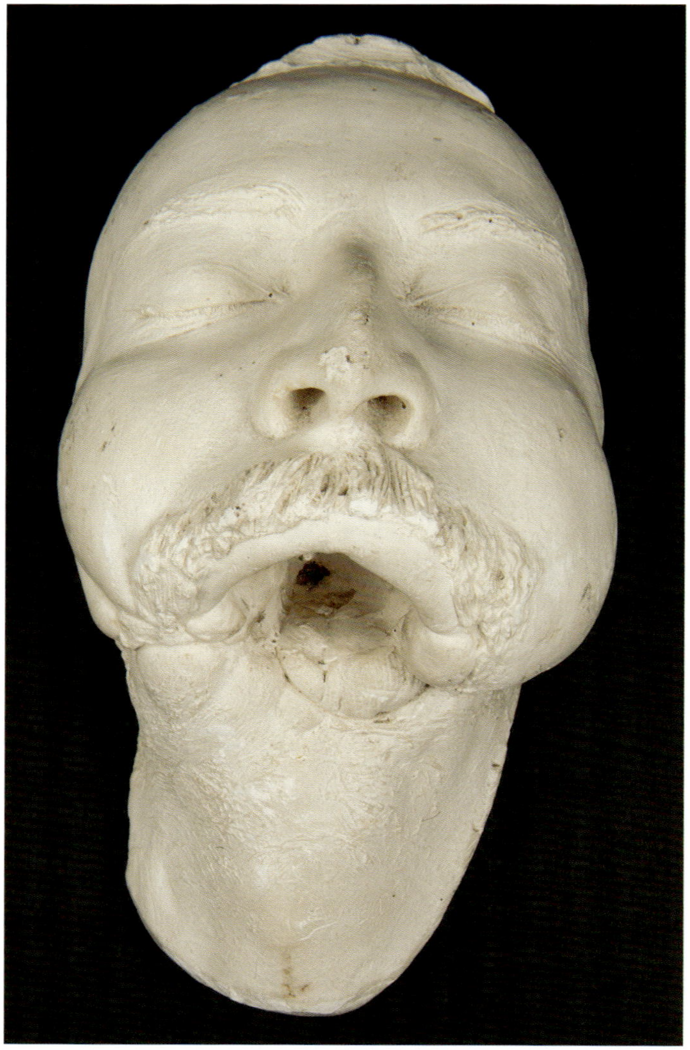

C. Morel. Facial mold. Quarlerland. 2018.2001.2.2. May 20, 1917. Plaster, 10" x 7" x 6."
National Museum of Health and Medicine, Silver Spring, Maryland.

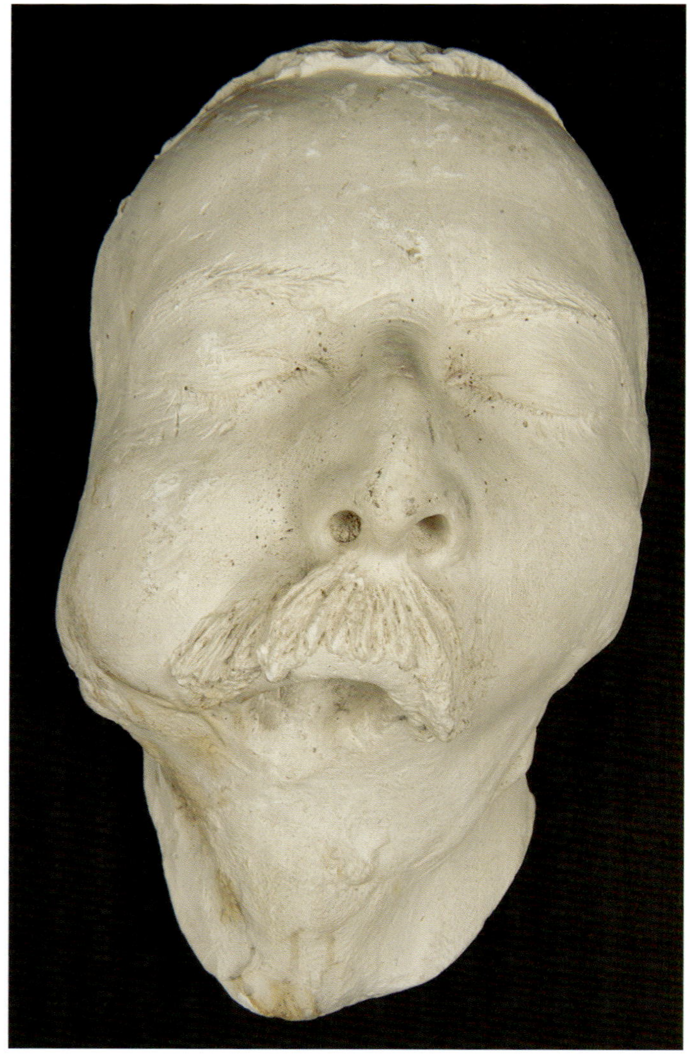

Unknown. Hammond maxillofacial splint with internal nasal support. M-550.10172. [1918]. Wire & red rubber, 12" x 9" x 8." National Museum of Health and Medicine, Silver Spring, Maryland.

Unknown. Red Cross Work on Mutilés (Mutilated Soldiers), Paris. Anna Coleman Ladd. 1918. 4-minute film. National Museum of Health and Medicine, Silver Spring, Maryland.

Ecole Dentaire de Paris. Plaster mode. with full lower dental splint replacing left molars. Dispensaire Militaire 45. (Military Dispensary #45) Ecole Dentaire de Paris (Dental School of Paris). M-550-10134. [1918]. Plaster, metal, 7" x 5" x 3." National Museum of Health and Medic ne, Silver Spring, Maryland.

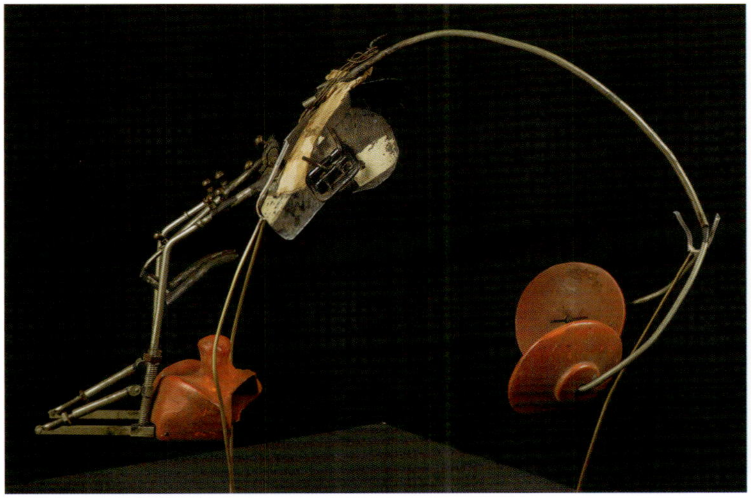

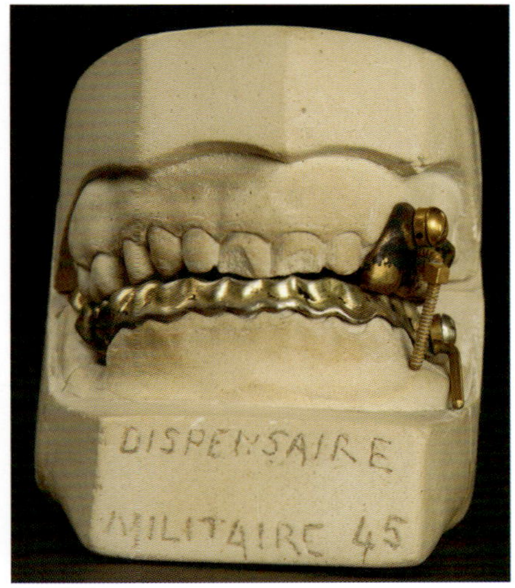

AMINA MENIA'S TRANS-MEDITERRANEAN AESTHETICS

Beth Hinderliter
Visiting Associate Professor
James Madison University

"Believe me, the zombies are more terrifying than the settlers,"

—Frantz Fanon, *Wretched of the Earth*

LEFT

Amina Menia, installation view *Monuments in Exile: An Infinite Page of Marble Writing*, 2019.

Beth Hinderliter is a visiting associate professor at James Madison University in the School of Art, Design and Art History and in Cross-Disciplinary Studies, which includes African, African American, and Diaspora Studies and Women's, Gender, and Sexuality Studies.

It started with a crack. The concrete "sarcophagus" built to enclose Paul Landowski's WWI memorial in central Algiers began to break apart in 2012. Designed by M'hamed Issiakhem to conceal the colonial monument before the occurrence of the Pan-African games in 1978, the concrete sarcophagus had been executed quickly. While many colonial monuments had been taken back to France or later repatriated, some, like Landowski's *Monument aux Morts* (Fig. 1), remained in Algiers, and at times, were partially dismantled or redecorated in the process of decolonization.

When the crack appeared in 2012, it arrived during the celebrations of Algeria's 50th anniversary of independence from France. The ghosts of the colonial past seemed to be trying to break free from their grave. For Amina Menia, the appearance of the crack—first small and later revealing the original monument underneath—was "like a bombshell." This explosion of shock captured her attention: she had never thought about working on a project dealing with Issiakhem, whose rigid socialist-realist style made him seem to this later generation of artists to be an "apparatchik." Her description of the explosive return of the colonial undead—those which could not be repatriated to France—is a kind of colonial trauma, a repetition, a reverberation of the shell shock into the future. It was the shelling that killed a majority of soldiers in WWI, not the invention of many new weapons, such

Fig. 1
"Post card of P. Landowski's *Monument aux Morts*, Algiers, 1939," included in Amina Menia's *Enclosed*, 2014.

as flame throwers and poison gas. Issiakhem had also experienced this shock when a bomb blew up in his hand when he was a child during WWII, leaving him with one arm for the rest of his life. This kind of explosion was notably feared by soldiers, who, like Sargent Paul Dubrulle, found the shelling to be the worst thing to fear in the Great War. He wrote during the battle of Verdun in 1916 that "to die from bullets seems to be nothing, parts of our being remain intact. But to be dismembered, torn to pieces, reduced to pulp, this is a fear that flesh cannot take" (Dubrulle 1917).

For those grieving their loved ones lost during in the war, death by explosion meant no marked burial site to visit. Approximately thirty percent of those who had been killed in the war had no remains identified. Even for those soldiers who were identifiable after being given hasty battlefield burials, the French National Commission on Military Burials took two post-war years to pass legislation that would remove the bodies and then send them home. The government mandated the importance of equality in death of its soldiers. As historians Jay Winter and Bruno Cabanes have detailed, the massive scale of death and the irrelevance of traditional grieving practices required the creation of new forms of memorialization, and a veritable industry of memorialization took hold as over 36,000 war memorials were erected across metropolitan France and its colonized territories. Landowski's monument in Algiers, like many others, sought to refuse the anonymity of mass death, yet it, like many others erected in France's colonial territories, represented metropolitan practices and cultural norms (Kidd 2002).

Landowski, who is perhaps best known as the sculptor of Rio de Janeiro's *Christ the Redeemer*, included in his monument a sculpted figure of an Algerian *spahi* (mounted soldier) alongside a French cavalryman. Together, along with a figure of Winged Victory, they held aloft the wounded body of a soldier. Despite the figures' collective effort here to honor the dead, both Algerian and French together (often referred to in that time as a *union sacrée* of colonizer and colonized), the French population largely ignored this symbolism, as the monument increasingly came to function for the French to honor only French lives lost. As Dónal Hassett has noted, just two years after its inauguration in 1930, the monument was used as a starting point for a race honoring the centennial celebration of Algerian colonization, effectively renouncing its supposed embodiment of a "fraternity of arms" (Hassett 2018).

Yet, these monuments, which did pay homage to Algerian war dead despite overt French stylization and propaganda, were often problematic to deal with in the decolonial era, as opposed to other monuments with explicit celebrations of French domination. The Algerians who had fought and died for France in WWI or WWII were not treated as traitors to their nation like the *harkis* who fought with France during the war of independence. Instead, they were seen as victims of colonial oppression and brutality and their suffering needed remembering. Hence, the solution of the entombment of Landowski's monument, which had been too large to send back to France, was preferable to its destruction. Encased in a robe of concrete and decorated with a pair of fists breaking free from its shackles, the *union sacrée*, long seen as propagandistic cover for France's keenness to sacrifice the lives of colonial soldiers, was effectively buried (Fig. 2).

For Menia, the crack's appearance in Issiakhem's monument during the 50th anniversary of independence was significant. She visited Issiakhem's sister, learning that he had been a part of the resistance during the war for liberation. She attempted to document the monument's disrepair but was repeatedly turned away by police who were guarding it. She took photos (Fig. 3). In them, you can see through the scaffolding. The face of a helmeted French soldier looks out—the dead had come back to life. She interviewed Bourdine Moussa, an artist who assisted Issiakhem during the decoration of Algiers for the Pan-African Games. He announced that repairing the crack in the monument was a bad idea. "We must

Fig. 2
"The Monument by M'hamed Issiakhem," photographed by Amina Menia, 2012. Included in Amina Menia, *Enclosed*, 2014.

remove this coffering. We must remove it and that's that. People have to deal with it. It won't bite them," he told her.

Had anything changed over the course of the thirty-four years that the Landowski memorial had been invisible? Despite the government's commitment to repair Issiakhem's monument, thereby continuing to hide the Landowski memorial, Menia sought in her work *Enclosed* to put the two artists into dialogue. Her work existed, as she wrote, in tracing the "footprint" of the crack in the monument, a crack which opened up interlocking memories, perspectives from both sides of the Mediterranean. It was a moment to seek what had changed since that first decade of decolonization. However, as recently as 2005, a French law (later rescinded) compelled French school curriculum to

Fig. 3
Amina Menia, *Les Martyrs reviennent cette semaine*, 2012. (titled after a novela by Tahar Ouettar, 1974) included in Amina Menia, *Enclosed*, 2014.

treat the history of colonialism positively. The heroic sacrifices of the French army were, under this law, to be given the honor that was seen as due to them. In response, the FLN (National Liberation Front) demanded that France must acknowledge "its crimes against Algerians." Indeed, the more France has been embroiled in *guerres de mémoires* over how different segments of the French population remember and historicize colonization and slavery, the more Algerians have pushed to get France to recognize its crimes (Fleming 2017). As historian Benjamin Stora remarked on the occasion of the 50th anniversary of Algerian independence, "time is not sufficient to make the wounds on both sides disappear. We see that the more time passes, the more memory returns" (Algeria Celebrates 2012).

Within the crack, the dead reappear, similar in many ways to the famous "The March of the Dead" scene in Abel Gance's 1919 film *J'Accuse*. Using montage and other forms of editing, Gance depicted soldiers' corpses rematerializing on a WWI battlefield. After they are reanimated, the semi-transparent ghosts plan to return to their homes and villages to ascertain if their sacrifices were made in vain. So, too in Tahar Ouettar's *Les Martyrs reviennent cette semaine* (1974), those who lost loved ones in the Algerian war for independence face survivor's guilt and pledge to create a freedom worthy of their sacrifice. Fear of judgement by the dead propel the living to extend their dedication and commitment to the task of building a better future. Frantz Fanon once asked what was scarier: a zombie or a colonial settler? Perhaps the governmental response to the crack in Issiakhem's monuments tells us the answer—a zombie settler? Landowski's figures are vengeful conquerors, who must be returned to their graves.

For her part, Menia finds the crack of this layered monument to be a basis for a future trans-Mediterranean writing of history. She tells us of the ways in which a city can molt, shedding its past like an "urban reptile" losing its skin. For her installation *Monuments in Exile: An Infinite Page of Marble Writing*, commissioned for *Colonial*

Fig. 4
Amina Menia, installation view *Monuments in Exile: An Infinite Page of Marble Writing*, 2019.

Wounds/Postcolonial Repair, she investigates the remembrance of WWI memorials at the time of the war's centennial (Fig. 4). In her travels across Algeria, Menia documents how monuments in cities like Oran, Mascara, Mostaganem, Sid, and Constantine have been transformed or dismantled, with parts often being sent by the French back to the metropole (Fig. 5). Whether they were transformed, demolished, or exiled, the monuments show us how the original purposes of these sites of memory have been subverted and new stories, those largely excluded from earlier official remembrances, are now told. In the gallery, shadows cast from five sculptural bases of monuments from across Algeria creep up the wall. As Menia calls it, they have lost their heads. The sculptures that were removed from the original monuments are drawn on the opposing wall and float above the shadows, never quite able to touch down and find a new base. The monuments themselves are stark and white, without decoration or inscribed text. This mirrors how these sculpted remains in Algeria are carefully cared for by the state, with all graffiti or disrepair quickly dealt with by a coat of new paint or marble cladding. They take up their place in the city as a blank page, a placeholder

Fig. 5
Amina Menia, Repurposed monument, Mostagnem. Photograph. 2019.

Fig. 6
Amina Menia, Monument stripped of sculpture and plaques, Oran. Photograph. 2018.

Fig. 7
Amina Menia, Monument base painted white, Sig. Photograph. 2018.

for the future yet to be. Within the gallery in miniature form, the monuments call to their missing parts across an ocean of darkness. Each have found new lives apart from, yet rooted in, past meanings.

According to Albert Camus, the Algerian city of Oran was never lacking in monuments: "The city has its account of marshals of Empire, ministers, and local benefactors," he wrote. "We meet them on small dusty plazas, resigned to the rain, like the sun, transforming themselves into stone with boredom" (Camus 1959,

Fig. 8
Postcard with view of the *Monument aux Morts* in Sig, Algeria. Undated.

Fig. 9
Amina Menia, Still from *A Peculiar Family Album*, 2012.

70). One monument in Oran, documented by Menia in her research, counters Camus' colonial plentitude with absence. All that remains is an empty pedestal, covered in graffiti, and surrounded by trash (Fig. 6). Where did the monument go? For the sculptures that remained, particularly the figural ones, many have been since repeatedly defaced or even dynamited.

In contrast with this pedestal located near Oran's train station which has accumulated urban debris and invites city residents to sit at its base, the remains of a monument in Sig gleam with fresh paint (Fig. 7). It is a blank slate, awaiting inscription and a return to commemoration.

Menia traces the routes of some monuments repatriated to France, where they acquired new meanings and often were dedicated to the approximately one million French returning from Algeria after its independence. In Lyon, a city where many *pieds-noirs* settled in the 1960s, the *Monuments aux Morts* from Oran was installed in 1968 with an inscription: "welcoming the children of North Africa." Another monument in Oran, a column memorializing the colonial battle of Sidi Brahim (1845), was partially dismantled with one figure being sent to the French city of Périssac, near Bordeaux. Similarly, Mostaganem's figural components of the *Monuments aux Morts*, two Algerian *tirailleurs*—were sent to Montpellier where they rest today facing the Museum of the Army.

Images from the colonial archives mix with present day depictions of Algerian cities in Menia's work. Colonial post cards with views of city squares and their *Monuments aux Morts* (Fig. 8) contrast with present day documentation of these same spaces. Archival strategies in contemporary art have sought to reveal the extent to which colonialism operated through a kind of "archival fever" in which the collection and control of information is equated with the capacity to dominate an adversary. Artists who have engaged colonial archives question their stability as a means of documenting and recording the past. For her part, Menia asks what are the master narratives found in the archives, and how can contemporary narratives and images rub these master narratives against the grain. In linking the many histories, emotions, and/or violence associated with a monument and the urban spaces it occupies, Menia works against the erasure of memory and to bridge temporal and spatial gaps. As she remarks in the voice-over narration in the video *A Peculiar Family Album,* she is fascinated by how there can be several cities in one city. Algiers, she says, is "an archipelago city," whose inhabitants appropriate its history, turning it modern, alive, and bustling (Fig. 9). Her works brought together for this exhibition share this fascination for subverting urban space and its dominant histories and narratives. Together they tell a postcolonial narrative rooted in witnessing, if not repairing, the wounds of the past in order to build for the future.

References

Algeria Celebrates 50 years of independence from France, 06/07/2012. France 24 https://www.france24.com/en/20120706-algeria-celebrates-fifty-years-independence-france-photos-war

Camus, Albert. 1959. *Noces Suivi de l'Été*. Paris: Gallimard.

Dubrulle, Paul. 1917. *Mon Régiment dans la fournaise de Verdun et dans la Bataille de la Somme: impressions de guerre d'un prêtre-soldat*. Paris: Plon.

Fleming, Crystal. 2017. *Resurrecting Slavery: Racial Legacies and White Supremacy in France*. Philadelphia: Temple University Press.

Hassett, Dónal. 2018. "A Tale of Two Monuments: The War Memorials of Oran and Algiers and Commemorative Culture in Colonial and Post-Colonial Algeria." in *Commemorating Race and Empire in the Great War Centenary*, edited by Shanti Sumartojo and Ben Wellings, 151-168. Liverpool: Liverpool University Press.

Kidd, William. 2002. "Representation or recuperation? The French Colonies and 1914–1918 War Memorials." In *Promoting the Colonial Idea: Propaganda and Vision of Empire in France*, edited by Tony Chafer and Amanda Sackur, 184-194. London: Palgrave Macmillan.

Smith, Leonard. 2014. *The Embattled Self: French Soldiers' Testimony of the Great War*. Ithaca: Cornell University Press.

ABOUT THE AUTHORS

Amina Menia (b. 1976) is a contemporary artist who questions the relationship of architecture to historical spaces and who challenges conventional notions around the exhibition space. Her artworks are crossovers of sculptures and installations that trigger an interaction between viewers and passersby and socio-spatial configurations. She has shown her work nationally and internationally, including at the Museum of Modern Art (Algiers), the Royal Hibernian Academy (Dublin), the Centre Georges Pompidou (Paris), the Museum of African Design (Johannesburg), the Museum of Contemporary Art (Marseilles), and the Marta Herford Museum (Herford, Germany). She participated in the 11th Sharjah Biennial (UAE), the Bienal de la Imagen en Movimiento (Buenos Aires), the Dakar Biennial 2014 (Senegal), the Folkestone Triennial 2014 (UK), and the 2015 Bruges Triennial. She spent a long-term residency in the city of Marseilles, working on the common architectural heritage of Algiers and Marseilles through the inspiring figure of the architect Fernand Pouillon.

The three works on exhibition in *Colonial Wounds/ Postcolonial Repair* represent her critique and analysis of the legacy of French colonialism. *Enclosed* (2012–ongoing) is a documentary-based installation that shows how the Algerian artist M'hamed Issiakhem circumvented his commission to "hide" the former French colonial Monument to the Dead of Algiers. He encased it in a temporary cement coffering but years later the casing cracked open. Her film, *A Peculiar Family Album* (2012), retrieves archival footage of the construction of public housing projects commissioned by then French Deputy-Mayor of Algiers Jacques Chevallier and designed by architect Fernand Pouillon. Her voice-over throughout the film analyzes this "housing battle" that emerged at the onset of the Algerian War of Independence (1954–1962). Her new installation created especially for James Madison University's Duke Hall Gallery of Fine Art, *Monuments in Exile: An Infinite Page of Marble Writing* (2019), analyzes the legacy of colonialism through monuments that have been abandoned, damaged, or re-purposed.

Maureen G. Shanahan is professor of art history at James Madison University in the School of Art, Design and Art History. She is a specialist on French modernism, the visual culture of World War I, trauma theory, and her research investigates gender, sexuality, and colonial discourse. She is completing a book entitled *The Colorist Doctor: Fernand Léger and the Aestheticization of Trauma*, which is currently under advanced review at a university press and which will analyze Léger's art in the context of individual and collective trauma. She is co-editor of *Simón Bolívar as National Myth and Cultural Sign* (University Press of Florida 2016), which examines the history of Bolívar as a contested cultural symbol of national identity and revolutionary politics. The *Colonial Wounds/Postcolonial Repair* exhibition arises out of her current research on photography about the French colonial soldier and worker during and after World War I. This research has been supported by a National Endowment for the Humanities summer seminar award in 2014, the inaugural Florence Gould Foundation Fellowship for French art and visual studies at the Sterling and Francine Clark Art Institute in 2015, and a Fulbright Award to France in 2017. Her forthcoming article, "The Battle for Hearts and Minds: The Nogent Mosque during World War I," will appear in a special issue of *African Arts* scheduled for summer/fall 2019.

Beth Hinderliter is a visiting associate professor at James Madison University in the School of Art, Design and Art History and in Cross-Disciplinary Studies, which includes African, African American, and Diaspora Studies and Women's, Gender, and Sexuality Studies. From 2008–2017, she taught at SUNY Buffalo State as an associate professor, where she also served as coordinator of African and African American Studies. Her current co-edited book project, *More than our Pain: Affect and Emotion in the Black Lives Matter Movement*, considers the role of emotions from rage and joy to grief in the contemporary human rights movement in the U.S., finding within emotions and affect the parameters for community coherence today as well as the footprint for a more equitable future society. She is interested in current activist image practices which give witness to present events while registering centuries of trauma. Her last co-edited volume *Communities of Sense: Rethinking Aesthetics and Politics* (Duke University Press 2008) also investigates issues of community formation via discussions of recent political theory and contemporary art and architectural practices.

EXHIBITION CHECKLIST

Lt. Albert Moreau. Group of wounded North African soldiers holding postcards. Jardin Colonial, Nogent-sur-Marne. 1916. Photograph. Établissement de Communication et de Production Audiovisuelle de Défense (ECPAD), France.

Jules Gervais-Courtellemont. *Tirailleurs Algériens*. Autochrome published in *Les Champs de bataille* (Paris, 1915), 47.

Unknown. French colonial soldiers as prisoners of war in a German P.O.W. camp. *Der Grosse Krieg in Bildern*, vol. 4 (1915), 32. Photography album.

Georges Scott. *La Breche* (1915) published in French periodical, *L'Illustration*. Original at Musée de l'Armée, Paris.

Sgt. J.J. Owens. Chemical Burns. Sgt. Thomas S. Davis. American Red Cross Hospital No. 6. OHA 229.38.25, Box 47, folder 3. October 4, 1918. Watercolor, 18" x 13." National Museum of Health and Medicine, Silver Spring, Maryland.

Auguste and Louis Lumière. Jean Bon, F29. OHA 367.16.001, Box 16. [1918] Color lantern slide, 4 ¾" x 3 ⅝." National Museum of Health and Medicine, Silver Spring, Maryland.

Auguste and Louis Lumière. Leonard Legarton, H2, side profile. OHA 367.16.002, Box 16. [1918] Color lantern slide, 4 ¾" x 3 ⅝." National Museum of Health and Medicine, Silver Spring, Maryland.

Auguste and Louis Lumière. Leonard Legarton, H2, frontal view. OHA 367.16.003, Box 16. [1918] Color lantern slide, 4 ¾" x 3 ⅝." National Museum of Health and Medicine, Silver Spring, Maryland.

Auguste and Louis Lumière. Paul Etienne, C10. OHA 367.16.004, Box 16. [1918] Color lantern slide, 4 ¾" x 3 ⅝." National Museum of Health and Medicine, Silver Spring, Maryland.

Unknown. Front and profile views of unknown African American soldier with facial scarification. OHA 264.001.076, page 76 of 251-page album. [1918]. Photography album, 8.5" x 14" x 1.5." National Museum of Health and Medicine, Silver Spring, Maryland.

Inez Demonet O'Brien. Facial reconstruction surgery diagram. Pvt. H.H. wounded on 10/4/1918, operation 4/11/1919. OHA 229.07.18, Box 11, folder 4. 1919. Pencil, watercolor, black ink, 15" x 11." National Museum of Health and Medicine, Silver Spring, Maryland.

Helen Ely Richardson. Facial reconstruction surgery diagram. John Foster I and II (4/14/1919 & 5/16/1919). 1919. Black ink drawing & red pencil, 10" x 13." National Museum of Health and Medicine, Silver Spring, Maryland.

Helen Ely Richardson. Facial reconstruction surgery diagram. John Foster III (5/31/1919). OHA 229.21.07, Box 25, folder 12. 1919. Black ink drawing & red pencil, 10" x 15." National Museum of Health and Medicine, Silver Spring, Maryland.

Unknown. Catastrophic Loss of both lower legs. OHA 229.26.22, Box 32, folder 3. [1918]. Watercolor on board, 10.5" x 12." National Museum of Health and Medicine, Silver Spring, Maryland.

F.E. Prior. #2 of 7 in a series of medical illustrations of thigh amputation. OHA 229.16.21. [1918]. Black ink on paper, 7" x 7." National Museum of Health and Medicine, Silver Spring, Maryland.

F.E. Prior. #6 of 7 in a series of medical illustrations of thigh amputation. OHA 229.16.21. [1918]. Black ink on paper, 7" x 7." National Museum of Health and Medicine, Silver Spring, Maryland.

Roy Reeve. Tong traction. French soldier (F.A. Treval) at American Red Cross Military Hospital 2. OHA 80 Reeve 13320A. [1918]. Photograph and black ink on card, 13.5" x 9." National Museum of Health and Medicine, Silver Spring, Maryland.

Sgt. J.J. Owens. Fractured Femur and Steinman pin. OHA 229.38.16. November 1, 1918. Watercolor, color pencil, black ink, 14" x 17." National Museum of Health and Medicine, Silver Spring, Maryland.

Roy Reeve. Diagram of Balkan Frame. OHA 366. Reeve 68.2. [1918]. Print of glass plate negative on photo paper, 3.5" x 4." National Museum of Health and Medicine, Silver Spring, Maryland.

Sgt. J.J. Owens. Side view of right gangrened foot. Sgt. Arthur McArthur. 1st Co., 369th Infantry. American Red Cross Military Hospital No. 5 & No. 2. OHA 229.39.01, Box 49, folder 4. October 4, 1918. Drawing and watercolor, 13" x 18." National Museum of Health and Medicine, Silver Spring, Maryland.

Sgt. J.J. Owens. Front view of left gangrened foot. Sgt. Arthur McArthur. OHA 229.38.18, Box 46, folder 12. November 29, 1918. Drawing and watercolor, 17" x 14." National Museum of Health and Medicine, Silver Spring, Maryland.

Unknown. Decoration ceremonies. Film 14.18 B 646. 1917–1918. 4-minute extract. Établissement de Communication et de Production Audiovisuelle de Défense (ECPAD), France.

Unknown. Wounded French soldiers. Film 14.18 B 730. 1917. 12-minute newsreel. Établissement de Communication et de Production Audiovisuelle de Défense (ECPAD), France.

C. Morel. Facial mold. Quarlerland. 2018.2001.2.1. Late 1916. Plaster, 10" x 7" x 6." National Museum of Health and Medicine, Silver Spring, Maryland.

C. Morel. Facial mold. Quarlerland. 2018.2001.2.2. May 20, 1917. Plaster, 10" x 7" x 6." National Museum of Health and Medicine, Silver Spring, Maryland.

Unknown. Hammond maxillofacial splint with internal nasal support. M-550.10172. [1918]. Wire & red rubber, 12" x 9" x 8." National Museum of Health and Medicine, Silver Spring, Maryland.

Ecole Dentaire de Paris. Plaster model with full lower dental splint replacing left molars. Dispensaire Militaire 45. (Military Dispensary #45) Ecole Dentaire de Paris (Dental School of Paris). M-550-10134. [1918]. Plaster, metal, 7" x 5" x 3." National Museum of Health and Medicine, Silver Spring, Maryland.

Unknown. *Red Cross Work on Mutilés (Mutilated Soldiers), Paris.* Anna Coleman Ladd. 1918. 4-minute film. National Museum of Health and Medicine, Silver Spring, Maryland.

[Corp. John Butler AEF]. Pvt. Alex G. Nesbit, 363d Infantry, Dijon, France. High explosive shell wound of face, OHA 229.27.20. October 8, 1918. Color pencil drawing, 16" x 11." National Museum of Health and Medicine, Silver Spring, Maryland.

Corp. John Butler AEF. Pvt. Alex G. Nesbit, 363d Infantry, Dijon, France. High explosive shell wound of face, OHA 229.27.20. October 29, 1918. Color pencil drawing, 12.5" x 11." National Museum of Health and Medicine, Silver Spring, Maryland.

Unknown. Facial reconstruction patient. Ahmed Bouziane. OHA 213.5-Leach Scrapbook. 1916, Photograph on original album page, 11" x 6 ¾." National Museum of Health and Medicine, Silver Spring, Maryland.

Amina Menia. *Enclosed*. 2012. Book documenting installation. Courtesy of the artist.

Amina Menia. *A Peculiar Family Album*. 2012. Video installation, single-channel, sound, loop (English voice over). Courtesy of the artist.

Amina Menia. *Monuments in Exile: An Infinite Page of Marble Writing*. 2019. Black chalk, plaster models. Courtesy of the artist.

ACKNOWLEDGEMENTS

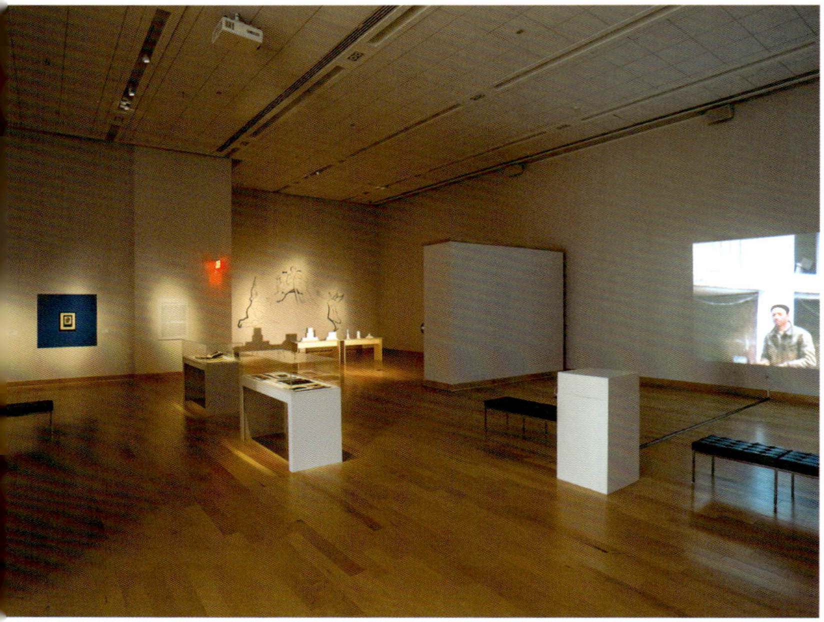

We would like to thank the many funders and supporters of *Colonial Wounds/Postcolonial Repair.* Planning and funding for exhibitions are often a multi-year process. We are very grateful to the members of three crucial committees that approved the exhibition and the bulk of its funding: the committee of the Duke Hall Gallery of Fine Arts, which approved the exhibition in fall 2017; the 2017–2018 College of Visual and Performing Arts (CVPA) Diversity Committee, which approved our application for the $10,000 Cultural Connections grant; and the 2017–2018 Dorothy Liskey Wampler Committee of the School of Art, Design and Art History (SADAH), which approved funds to bring our guest artist, Amina Menia. In addition to the CVPA, the College of Arts and Letters, and the College of Science and Mathematics contributed funding. We are also very grateful to the many offices, programs, and departments that supported the exhibition and catalog production: the Office of Access and Inclusion; Biology; the Center for Global Engagement; Cross-Disciplinary Studies (including Africana Studies, Film Studies, Middle East Communities & Migrations, and Women & Gender Studies); English; Health Sciences; Justice Studies; Modern Languages; and the School of Media Arts and Design. These units have helped us promote the exhibition and its coordinated events with their students, staff, and faculty, thus expanding our audience across the campus and into the community.

Throughout the past two years, the exhibition has received widespread support throughout the SADAH community. Students in Maureen G. Shanahan's exhibition seminar contributed their engagement in and enthusiasm for the themes of the seminar and guided visitors on the day of the opening. Many gallery interns and assistants have made important contributions. Martha Hemingway has been a tireless, exacting, and consistently excellent researcher and gallery assistant. Graduate student Carlson Jenkins and undergraduate Vilma Castro contributed their labor in preparing Amina Menia's installation. Oumaima Azzat designed the poster. Graduate student Chris Cohen assisted in the collection and transportation of loaned objects. Mark Dowdy used his technological wizardry in the installation of all the films and Mark Rooker in making a support structure for the maxillofacial splint. Carissa Henriques has provided her graphic design expertise for a nominal fee. Dr. Sarah Brooks, art history area coordinator, provided advice and insights from her exhibition experiences as well as advocacy throughout. Our director, Dr. Kathy Schwartz, has provided her unfailing positive energy and supplemental funding for the catalog. We are especially grateful for the generous advice and expertise of John Ros, Director of the Duke Hall Gallery of Fine Arts, and Dr. Laura Katzman, Professor of Art History. Their wise counsel has helped us produce a polished, professional result; any flaws are our own.

Many institutions and individuals very generously provided their images and artwork with little to no cost. Amina Menia, our guest artist, has been a pleasure to work with; she has permitted publication of her images in this catalog without cost. The National Museum of Health and Medicine in Silver Spring, Maryland, and its staff have been incredibly generous in opening up their archives, lending materials, providing a private behind-the-scenes tour for our students, and advising us throughout. The French Army's film and photography archives, the ECPAD, has been similarly generous, by providing little-known film and photography at a minimal cost.

Finally, we wish to thank the poets who remembered our soirées: Adéró̩nké Adésànyà and Sofia Samatar.